TRIBAL WOMEN EMPOWERMENT AND GENDER ISSUES

Tribal Women Empowerment and Gender Issues

ZENAB BANU

KANISHKA PUBLISHERS, DISTRIBUTORS
NEW DELHI-110 002

KANISHKA PUBLISHERS, DISTRIBUTORS
4697/5-21A, Ansari Road, Daryaganj
New Delhi -110 002
Phones : 2327 0497, 2328 8285
Fax : 011-2328 8285
E-mail : kanishka_publishing@yahoo.co.in

First Published: 2001
Second Edition: 2011

ISBN : 978-81-7391-389-7

PRINTED IN INDIA

Published by Madan Sachdeva for Kanishka Publishers, Distributors, 4697/5-21A, Ansari Road, Daryaganj, New Delhi-110 002, Typeset by Sunshine Graphics, Delhi, and Printed at Rajdhani Printers, Delhi.

Preface

In all societies, there are differences in power between persons. There is not a single society where all adults have exactly the same influence over every decision where everyone has exactly the same rights and duties. Social differentiation and equalities are, in other words universal phenomenon. The power of man as against woman, likewise is not the same. There is a theory of power, if it is equally distributed, it ceases to be power. The difference between the gender are several. Power is given by the society and this makes difference in gender. There are two fundamental different ways of regarding gender differences. On the one hand, there are certain biological differences between man and woman; the genitals look different and function differently. It is precisely what we call sex.

But the gender differences are due to social and cultural factors. The tribal society has its own history, its own structure and therefore the gender issue is constituted out of the tribal history and tribal structure. Viewed from this perspective the gender issues of caste, society and for that matter secular society are different from the tribal society. In other words though the tribal society is not homogenous its gender issues are different from the non-tribal society. The Seventy-Third Constitutional Amendment gives power to tribal women by way of reservation, and through protective and development safeguards. We have examined the gender issues found in the tribal society resulting from the restructuring of Panchayati Raj. While doing field work we have encountered another problem in the field of political empowerment given to tribal women. Admittedly tribal women have become victims of inefficiency because of their lack in education and modernisation, the implications of empowerment are much wider and abiding in this wider society. We find that though women suffer termination harassment, proxy domination, caste factionalism but outside the corridors of Panchayati Raj they have made a breakthrough in their day-to-day life. In the wider society unlike their non-tribal counterparts they face lesser problems. It appears that the tribal women today are passing through the stage of transition so far the wielding of Panchayati Raj is concerned. There awaits a hopeful future for the tribal women of scheduled area.

Field work for the present enquiry was done during the year 1999-2000. The field consisting of the districts of south Rajasthan which constitute the only sub-plan area of the state. Besides Grasia, Damor and Mina, the Bhils constitute the only numerically dominant group in south Rajasthan. The situation of empowerment among the women focuses, therefore, on Bhils.

The study was sponsored by M.L. Sukhadia University, Udaipur. The author is indebted to the University.

At the close, thanks are due to our innumerable Panchs, Sarpanchs, Pradhans and Zila Pramukhs who in a candid way came forward to share their experiences with me. Officials also deserve my thanks for giving me the relevant literature and know-how about the functioning of Panchayati Raj. I am also indebted to my well-wisher and mentor, Dr. S.L. Doshi who gave me insight in the tribal life. I have benefited enough from his research work. My husband, Mansoor Ali and other family members deserve my sense of gratitude for helping me to conduct the field work and encouraging me to complete the work.

ZENAB BANU

Contents

CHAPTER 1

Theoretical Thrust

THEORETICAL THRUST

Empowerment has become a fashionable concept today. Earlier the term was used by political scientists. They used it in a very restricted sense. Normally by power they meant political power or usually the power politically assigned to an institution by the Constitution or administrative rules. Later on the concept became a tradition of the social sciences. With the coming of globalisation, empowerment is now being increasingly applied to the economically poor nations and the weaker and subaltern masses of people. In Third World countries we often speak about empowerment of the blacks, the backward and the wretched of the earth.

During the period from 1960s to 1970s there has been a tremendous rise of feminisation. All over Europe females have come against the male domination and patriarchy. As a matter of fact there has been an alliance between the women belonging to blacks and whites; in Third World countries between women belonging to subaltern groups and super ordinate groups, it is a war between male domination and inferiorisation.

In our country empowerment has assumed different dimension. We find its common use in two ways: empowerment of scheduled castes, scheduled tribes and women. The second meaning which is very popular with the government is the Seventy-Third Constitutional Amendment. The Panchayati Raj has given new powers to women at different tiers of the local government. It is very interesting to note that sociology and social anthropology have yet not used empowerment in terms of the "new development" attained by the weaker sections.

A quick check through dictionaries, encyclopaedias and glossaries of popular textbooks of political science shows that the term in itself is largely absent. By and large, 'the scholarly discussion of empowerment' has been context-driven rather than theory-driven. What is the context that brings the idea of empowerment so insistently to the attention of Indians today. In a nutshell, that context is the contradiction between a hierarchical social order and a democratic political system. To be sure, the contradiction was present and perceived even at the time of independence. But at that time it was hoped and believed that the contradiction would be inevitably ceased with the transfer of power from British to Indian hands. This does not happen and the contradiction has become, if anything, more acute, more extensive and more clearly perceived.

Power in the traditional Indian society has been hierarchically distributed. There is always much power with the men than with the women. As a result of this kind of unequal power distribution the Indian society has empirically become male dominated. There has been disabilities in society due to caste and gender inequalities. Democracy in this context is a new value structure which guarantees equal power to both the sexes. And thus, at least, in theory gender status does not suffer from unequal power distribution. But this is all in theory. When the Seventy-Third Constitutional Amendment came it became clear that there is desire to break the unequal power distribution between male and female. The amendment thus becomes a historical occurrence. It is in this context that empowerment has become a popular word among political scientists, sociologists, and media.

Diverse Meaning of Empowerment

As mentioned above, the use of empowerment as a conceptual framework is new. Defining its current meaning Andre Beteille[1] observes:

> Empowerment is about social transformation. It is about radical social transformation; and it is about the people—ordinary, common people, rather than politicians, experts and other socially or culturally advanced persons, *above all it is about power, although the concept of power contained in it is generally left unspecified.*
>
> *Empowerment is both a means to an end and an end in Itself.* (emphasis mine). The term adopts itself differently in situations and its significations is both variable and fluid.

Actually the idea of empowerment is drawn from the context of human rights. Human rights in this sense is broader. It included basic needs, economic security, capacity building, skill formation and dignifies social existence. The Indian Constitution has created several rights. It allows a large number of rights for all members of the society irrespective of their social and economic standing. The constitutional amendments give right to the weaker sections and particularly scheduled castes and scheduled tribes. Contextually, therefore, empowerment in Indian context stands for transformation of people belonging to weaker segments. It means that the hidden meaning of empowerment is not only political empowerment, but social and cultural empowerment also. In other words empowerment relates to social transformation among the women. The idea of empowerment is thus political, economic, social and cultural. It would be erroneous to think that empowerment consists only of political power. It is hoped that with the attainment of political power through Panchayati Raj, the women will also acquire economic and socio-cultural power. There are a large number of situations wherein decisions have to be made at the family, caste, village and regional levels. The empowerment given to women would effect all these levels of life.

Re-distribution of Power: Towards Social Rearrangement

The theory of power has been developed very elaborately in recent times. (We shall have to understand empowerment in wider context. What we are trying to do is to establish reciprocity between empowerment conceptualisation and empirical reality at the Panchayati Raj level). Such an approach to empowerment would on one hand enrich our theoretical formulations and on the other hand, an adequate understanding of social reality. We shall return to empowerment to women in Panchayati Raj Institutions, but before we do that let us look again at the definition of empowerment from linguistic structuralism. Recently the French structuralists have argued that the social structure draws heavily from linguistic structure. For these theorists language is symbolic. Language is power and therefore, when we say that there is empowerment of women we want to stress that *women have power of knowledge.* Such a proposition requires a little discussion.

In this context we would refer to Michel Foucault (1976) who says that power is nothing but knowledge. In other words those who have power have knowledge. On the basis of such an understanding of power and empowerment we would refer to some propositions which emerged from the writings of Foucault:[2]

1. Power is not something that is acquired, seized or shared, something that one holds on to or allows to slip away; power is exercised from innumerable points;
2. Relations of power are found in economic processes, knowledge relationships and sexual relations;
3. Powers come from below: that is, there is no binary and all encompassing opposition between rulers and ruled at the root of power relations. One must suppose that manifold relationships of force that take shape and come into play in the machinery of products in families, limited groups and institutions;
4. Power relations are both intentional and non-subjective.

We have mentioned the power propositions given by Foucault because these have greater relationship with our study. Foucault has argued that the sources of power are many. It means that power is not only derived from Seventy-Third Constitutional Amendment. This is one known source of power. But this source is multiplier. It opens up new sources of power, namely, family, caste, religion, village etc. Second proposition which assumes importance is the context of Indian society. Foucault argues that power relations are not only in terms of ruler and the ruled, the dominant and the subordinate. It is in fact, a network of social relations. Power is found in economy, knowledge and sex. For instance, the advocates of population controls now argue that if women are educated as in the case of Kerala, it would go a long way in population control. If they are aware about the complications which results from sex relations they can simply say 'no' to their husband. This is precisely the power of Panchayati Raj.

Yet another implication of power proposition as given by Foucault is that power is derived from below. It involves manifold relations of force. It includes the whole process of production, consumption. It is found in groups and institutions.

Foucault has given new dimension to power analysis. Such an analysis has wider implications in India. Andre Beteille argues that empowerment in Indian context has become much comprehensive. His observations run as below:[3]

> the most radical theories of empowerment are those that called for empowerment of the people as a whole. These are populist theories and they are mistrustful of institutions as such, because they sees that as obstacles to the aspiration of the ordinary people—peasants, workers, students, dalits, women—to secure control over their own lives. They ignore or reject the distinction that social theories have been at pains to make between naked power and legitimate authority. They believe that the well-being of institution is best secured by having full and equal participation by all in the conduct of their affairs, for the historically minded, the model of such institution is the Paris Commune of eighteenth century, once greatly admired by Marx.

When we talk about empowerment of women we are specific to the power given to women in Panchayati Raj. But the concept of empowerment is not restricted to only Panchayati Raj institutions. What we want to stress is that the meaning of empowerment is comprehensive. It is within Panchayati Raj but it goes beyond Panchayati Raj. The moment a tribal woman becomes *Zila Pramukh,* she immediately becomes a symbol of power for the women of the district as a whole. She immediately becomes a model of imitation and the political power trickles down to other areas of community's life. It is with this wider meaning of power and empowerment, power and authority that we look into the problem of our study. The study, in one stance is political; in another it is a gender issue, and further it is social, cultural and economic.

Deconstruction of Patriarchy

Recently post-modernity has stressed for a new theory in social sciences. The post-modern theorists such as Habarmas, Bourdeau and Derrida have advocated that the traditional and modern concepts fail to explain 'the new situations' which are fast appearing as a result of globalisation are falling into disrepute. Derrida vehemently talks about deconstruction. He says that the explicit and implicit interpretations of our age old macro theories are now put to challenge. Among such theories are some of the reputed theories of patriarchy and patriarchal domination. Women all over the world are challenging the domination exercised by males over the females. The gender problem which today occupies a sensitive and respectable status in social sciences challenges the exploitation of the patriarchy. Post-modernist theorists suggest for the deconstruction of patriarchical domination. The women have armed themselves to fight against male chauvinism. The view point of post-modernists is well expressed by Stephen Crook[4] in their post-modernisation work:

> modern societies are characterised by pronounced structural and categorical differentiation at the level of gender. Moreover the gender system is masculine dominated, that is, it involves the subordination of women by men. Although this is often treated as an undifferentiated structure of patriarchy, we preferred to see the masculine gender system of modernisation as a process of transformation between two phases, direct hierarchy and extended hierarchy, which are at least partly analogous to the transaction to product class to consumption status.

The approach taken by post-modern thinkers is altogether different. They do not think about empowerment of women in the public life. They assumed that women have an assured status in the political democracy. They also accept that at the level of production about which Marx talked much, the women have occupied a better place. What worries post-modernists is that women should also be given empowerment in the field of consumption. At the macro level or at the level of world order, such an approach seems to be logical. But India and also a large number of Third World countries are far behind in the realm of post-modernity. As a matter of fact the problem of empowering the women in countries like India involves a large number of societal sectors. We would, therefore, look at the problem of women empowerment with the social and political reality that we find in our country.

Gender Differentiation in Society

No society is without social differentiation. Inequality is the mark of society. In all societies, there are differences in power between persons. There is not a single society where all adults have exactly the same influence over every decision, where every one has exactly the same rights and duties. Social differentiation and inequality are, in other words, universal phenomena. The romantic ideas of the eighteenth and nineteenth centuries about the original primitive societies where all humans supposedly had the same rank and were political equals, was completely devastated when the first professional ethnographers return from the field. Even among the very small groups, and even among people with very simple technology, differential rank existed. Unlike what many 'armchair theorists' thought of small scale societies do not lack internal differentiation. Marx and Engels were thus right in assuming, in the mid-nineteenth century that there are universal criteria for social differentiation which are the distinctions between older and younger people, between man and woman and between insiders and outsiders, 'us' and 'them'.

Empowerment is a concept which carries certain elements. The concept of power which is prevalent in political science heavily draws from Max Weber. The advocates of power make a striking observation. They argue that the social differentiation which we get in society is lesser social and cultural and more political. As a matter of fact the situation of social stratification found in all the societies can we better explained by power. Perhaps Laski is the first modern political scientist who uses power and privilege as the decisive criteria for social differentiation. The division of labour which is used as a criterion for social stratification is a too narrow approach to the understanding of social inequality. It is worthwhile, therefore, to look at social differentiation from the perspective of power. Men and women are the two strata in society. They can be explained through the variable of power. If the society is divided by male and female, that is sex, it can be seen from gender point of view.

Power: Some Relevant Questions

True, power has become relevant today in the context of the upliftment of women. The constitution guarantees fundamentally not to discriminate against caste, creed and sex. Following the dictum, the government promoted a large number of programmes to improve the status of women. And to study the emergence of new status of women study cells at various levels of our institutions have been started. A large number of women NGOs have been started to promote the cause of women. All our efforts are directed to empower the women—socially, culturally, politically and economically. In such a situation it is worthwhile to ask: What is power? What are its manifestations? What are its sources? What is the legitimacy of power and what are the sanctions if the power is defied? The questions are relevant and need to be attended to.

Power: Social and Political

Literature on power is very rich in social sciences. As a matter of fact the political order in any society consists of those institutions within which men acquire, wield or influence distribution of power. Generally we ascribe 'power' to those who can influence the conduct of others even against their will. But such an understanding of power is quite simple the term is very ambiguous and requires further explanation. Power is also understood by influence, ability and a number of other such terms. If we really want to analyse power we shall have to explain it in scientific terms.

Where everyone is equal there is no politics, for politics involves subordinates and superiors. All institutional conduct, of course, involves distributions of power, but such distributions are the essence of politics. Insofar as it has to do with the state, the political order is the final authority; in it is instituted the final sanctions involving physical force over a given territorial domain. This trend marks of political institutions such as the state, from other institutional orders.

Whatever may be the nature of power—social or political, it implies an actor who can carry out his will and thereby getting submission to obedience. The general problem of politics accordingly is the explanation of varying distributions of power and obedience. One basic problem of political psychology is why men obey those who are powerful? This raises the problem of legitimacy. After all if there is power there is invariably a legitimacy to it. In other words, if women are given power, it implies that society and the people at large would give legitimacy to such power. Surely power has sanctions but if sanctions are not implemented, what would happen to power? Such an understanding of power requires a scientific approach.

Social scientists have made an elaborate attempt to analyse the concept of power. Longback MacIver, a political scientist and also a sociologist tried to clarify power. He argued that power has to be seen in community and in society, not in government or in the state. It is apparent furthermore, that not all power is political power and that political power—like economic, financial, industrial, and military power—is only one of several and various kinds of social power. Power, in short is a universal phenomenon in human societies and in all social relationship. It is never wholly absent from social interaction, except perhaps in the primary group where personal identification is incomplete and in those relations of polite acquaintance which are social in the narrowest sense. All other social relations contains components of power.

Power has several appendices. There is closest association between power and prestige. Perhaps the immediate cause of the location of power is prestige. E.S. Rose observes: 'the class that has the most prestige will have the most power or the class which has the most power will have the most prestige.' In the context of empowerment of tribal women naturally we shall have to analyse as to what extent women get prestige in terms of power they have.

Then there is the relationship between power and influence. It is said that influence and power occurs in relative isolation from each other and so also are relatively independent variables. We should say, for example, that Karl Marx has exerted incalculable influence upon the twentieth century, but this poverty stricken exile who spent so many of his hours in the British Museum was hardly a man of power. It is the ideas which are influential not the man. Stalin, on the other hand, is a man of influence only because he is first a man of power. Influence does not require power, and power may be dispensed with influence. Influence may convert a friend but power converts friends and foe alike. Influence attaches an idea, a doctrine, or a creed and has its locus in the ideological sphere. *Power attaches a person, a group, or an association, and has its locus in the social sphere.*

There is yet another need to distinguish power from dominance. Actually power's social-political dominance is psychological. The locus of power is in groups and it expresses itself inter-group relations; the locus of dominance is in the individual and it expresses itself in inter-personal relations. Power appears in the status of which people occupy in formal organisation; dominance in the roles they play in informal organisation. Power is a function of the organisation of association of the arrangement and juxtaposition of groups and of the structure of society itself. Dominance, on the other hand, is a function of personality or of temperament, it is a personal tract. Dominating individual play roles in powerless groups, submissive individuals in powerful ones. Some groups acquire an inordinate power. Specially in the political sense, because there are so many submissive individuals who are easily pursuant and who meekly confirmed to the norms which membership imposes.

Some Important Aspects of Power

In the preceding sections we have distinguished power from prestige, from influence and from dominance. We would say that power is not force. It is not authority. Biersted, a political sociologist gives three basic characteristics of power:

1. it is latent force,
2. it is manifest power, and
3. authority is institutionalised power.

Max Weber at another place has given three features of power:

1. organisation,
2. struggle for power, and
3. legitimacy.

All through his works Weber stresses that power has always some kind of organisation, whether it is a church or school. Power ceases to be power, if its legitimacy is challenged or defied and whether we see it or not, whether it is latent or manifest, there is always struggle to get more and more power. The chances of conforming to the power are greater if the source of power is genuine. If the people at large except to the power given to an institution or a person, legitimacy would come. On the other hand if the locus of power is fragile, the people would not conform to it and thus the power would loose its existence. When we look at the empowerment of women in the present study we shall have to apply a part of our theoretical framework to develop an insight in the power relations. In other words, if we give power to women from the source of the masses of people, there is possibility of its acceptance. But if the source of power is only statutorily, the chances of its legitimacy are vague and poor. But this is again only a theoretical hypothesis. We shall have to look into the empirical situation.

We have raised the problem of the source of power. But the sources are varied. There are various resources which give rise to power. Lewis Caus has provided a category of resources which give rise to power. He observes:[5]

> the resources that can be turned into power are varied. They may involve control over financial means or over means of coercion. They may consist in privileged excess to knowledge or the monopoly of excess to circles of persons possessing superior power. They may flow from privileged commerce with sacred beings or from magical abilities. They may stem from the ownership or control over means of production or over means of distribution. There are hence a great variety of power resources, so large a variety in effect to make it unprofitable to attempt at exhaustive enumeration. Social structures and historical periods, moreover differ as to the resources for the exercise of power that are most typically employed. In some societies and periods physical, coercive power may . . . the centre of the stage whereas in others the power that flows from the privilege position in the market place for goods and labour may be decisive.

Power: The Sources of Stratification

The studies recently taken up under the theme of gender have discussed social stratification in terms of power. Our argument is that if tribal women are empowered from statutory point of view it could also empower them economically and educationally.

Power itself is a strong variable in creating social stratification. The consequence of empowerment among the tribal women should result in reshaping the stratification of tribals. Thus empowerment of tribals, so far as our study is concerned, is in a matter of fact societal stratification also. Political empowerment thus has become a gender issue in the tribal society. It is again a popular approach in the study of women to talk about gender discrimination. Let us look at the meaning of gender issue.

Gender relations are of two kinds: biological and socio-cultural. When women are discriminated against men on the grounds of biological differentiation, it gives rise to gender issues. Thomas Hyllande Eriksen makes this differentiation quite striking as he writes:[6]

> there are two fundamentally different ways of regarding gender differences. On the one hand, there are certain biological differences between men and women; the genitals look different and function differently, women give birth to children, men usually have larger bodies, and so on. At this level, it is customary to use the term sex instead of gender.
>
> On the other hand, in practice gender differences are codified and institutionalised socially and culturally and it is largely this kind of differences which we focus on. It is distinguished from (biological) sex by the term gender.

All societies have some kind of gender differentiation. And all consider these differences quite vital. However, there are important variations in the ways the relationship between man and woman are worked out, and therefore, it is difficult to generalise about gender. *Gender can be studied as a relationship—man is defined in relation to woman and woman in relation to man*—and this relationship is conceived of differently in different society.

It is not new to study woman. In our country we have been engaged in women studies for longer part of our history. But this does not solve the problem with which women are confronted. True, there is illiteracy in women, they are poor; their life expectancy is shorter and above all they are backward. And similar is the situation of man. In fact most of the Asian countries are poor, illiterate and backward. We do not complain about it we have been conditioned so, historically. But the problem begins to get serious when we look at the backward status of women in comparison with man, the discrimination becomes serious. Here we look at empowerment from two basic perspectives. One, discrimination and two lower status in social stratification.

The gender differences are alright. Some of these are natural and should not give rise to any problem. But some of the gender differences are so acute that society has got them codified and institutionalised. These differences are social and cultural. For instance, in the field of our study, south Rajasthan the former princely state of Dungarpur had allowed legally the elopement of women among the Bhils. The women as if were meant to be taken away forcibly. Among the Gracias, a scheduled tribe, woman can be married without her consent and procreate children.

Why study the empowerment of women? What was the need to empower women? The questions are relevant. The feminist movement started in India, right from the sixties of twentieth century. The movement increasingly got speeded. It was common to find female foeticide and infanticide. There were political violence, women got marginalised and there was impoverishment of the majority of women within the transforming economy. There were disputes regarding inheritance over property. What is amazing is that the population explosion was explained in terms of the increased procreation of women. It was forgotten that in India sex relations with women are hardly taken with their permission. The decision to have sex in most of the cases is taken by the men. With this sex reality, the population explosion is made against women. Add to it the cases of dowry burning and injustices meted against women. It appears that the problem of empowering the women has been raised owing to the social and historical factors which have rendered women helpless. Power thus is specific to time and people. Empowerment of women in India, therefore, has to be seen in a wider context.

Theories of Power and Women

Not much has been written on the theories of power. Theory does not develop out of vacuum. Neither it is the result of man of 'great ideas', 'brilliant minds', or 'Astute observation'. Elizabeth Grosz very rightly observes about the origin and development of power theory:[7]

> Power theory is the product of history, and thus requires an understanding of the socio-political and intellectual context out of which theories and knowledge developed. It is the result of the interwoven and mutual defining set of relations between one theory or discourse and many others.

What Elizabeth Grosz argues that there is no authentic theory for women power. We have some metaphor only which expressed the need for a theory of power. Some of the feminists authors have made a stocktaking of the status of theory building in the field of gender relations. Most of them argue that the present set-up of feminist theories is based much on patriarchy and its related assumptions. Whether we look at the Zero-sum theory of power or other theories of power we immediately find that all these have a bias for patriarchy. What is needed today is to build a gender theory devoid of patriarchal assumptions. In some cases gender theories derive heavily from sex relations. Such a state of theories of power make it obligatory to develop a logical strategy for building a women power theory. Grosz has suggested for building such a viable theory. Her argument runs as below:[8]

> Feminist theory must always function in two directions if it to effectively challenge patriarchal knowledge. On the one hand, it must engage in what could be called a *negative* or *reactive* project—the project of challenging what currently exists or criticising what prevail, social, political and theoretical relations. Without this negative and anti-sexist goal, feminist theory remains ineffective and unrelated to socio-theoretical *status quo*.

The feminist theorists reiterate that we should immediately deconstruct all the theories pertaining to women and women power based on patriarchy. In social science theory building depends much on empirical grounding. Such a theory is based on data and method. Theory should not draw from patriarchal values. It should be in all possibility an unbiased theory.

Some Architects of Women Power Theory

The problem of empowerment of women has caught the attention of a new crop of theorists. These theorists have begun to look at the status of women from a new perspective. They are not monolith to look at the problem as we do in India only from political science perspective. It is our observation that recently most of the political scientists have taken to write on the theme of women empowerment. And all of them, perhaps without exception are writing on empowerment with reference to Panchayati Raj and Seventy-Third Amendment. For them there is no question of distribution of power beyond political institutions. It is all superficial. The problem has to be discussed with reference to the theory of power.

Althusser, Lacan, Foucault and Derrida are four French theorists whose works can be related if not to a common content, then at least to a common context, that of French Philosophy. Althusser challenges humanism, particularly Sartrean Version, by claiming that consciousness at best provides merely a subjective or personal view of reality. This personal view does not confirm to the objective reality. With this argument in mind that consciousness is subjective, Althusser rejects humanism. If we reduce Althusser to the empowerment of women in India we would only argue that if women are politically empowered they would get empowerment in other realms of life also. This is merely political subjective consciousness. Whether it is objectively true is a matter of further investigation.

Another aspect of Althusser's theory is the rejection of Marxian determinism. He does not accept that social and political conditions are determined by economic consideration. According to him these aspects of society get relative autonomy from economic relations. Elizabeth Grosz tries to establish that Althusser looks at women empowerment with a new perspective. This new perspective steams from ideology. Grosz's arguments run below:[9]

> His anti-humanism refuses any notion of a pre-given subjectivity free of ideology, and his anti-economism accords an autonomy to socio-cultural practices. Together these influence a surprisingly large number of feminists. Many saw in Marxist analyses of class relations a striking analogy with women's patriarchal operation.

As a matter of fact Althusser helped active feminists, even Marxist feminists, to the assumption that women's identities are somewhat natural. His anti-humanism and his account of the social construction of subjectivity in and by ideology propelled many feminists away from natural or biological accounts of women's identities towards social, cultural and historical explanations. The theory of Althusser on the problem of women empowerment alternatively rests on ideology. He takes a departure from the macro theories and shifts to ideology. While discussing ideology he relates it to power relations. According to him ideology is not simply a series of empirical events but a highly developed social structure. As social structure ideology distorts and obscures the existing power relations. His thesis propounds that ideology is a system of ideas, beliefs, practices and values that are obvious and natural.

The present day women empowerment is largely based on biological and natural qualities. The beauty contests as we find today all over India promote the natural gist of women and carry the ideology of dominant class. The French theorists argue that feminist should be examined with reference to social system and various other institutions. The bride burning, rape, violence against women, oppression of women and other such atrocities against women are nothing but class domination, patriarchal exploitation and capitalistic discrimination. These are some of the perspectives which emerge from the ideological framework given by Althusser. Lacan is another French theorist who is said to be the most controversial and charismatic psycho-analyst since Sigmund Freud. He presents a series of detailed readings Freud's text which have proved to be a major source of inspiration for Althusser's account of ideology, as well as for contemporary French feminism.

Lacan has criticised Freud's theory of sex on the strength of symbolic and imaginary interpretations. He links himself with linguistic structuralism. Actually Ferdinand de Saussure was a linguist. The new structuralism which has developed in France owes much to Saussure. Lacan works on the theme of structuralism. His theory has generated a good deal of controversy in feminists circle. Lacan is credited to provide an astute analysis of patriarchy. He argues that women can hardly be empowered if, their uplift rests on patriarchy. First, and above all any theory of women empowerment should say goodbye to patriarchy. Actually all efforts should be made to weaken patriarchy.

Foucault has analysed power with a different perspective. He came into prominence during the period after Althusser and Lacan were subjected to political criticism. In his earlier works he was influenced by linguistic structuralism and genealogy. At a latter stage Foucault became critical to Marxism as theory and practice. He claims that, Marxists have ignored the detailed operations of power by focusing largely on its global forms. As a result major manifestations of power are either ignored or politically minimised. As long as one posed the question of power while subordinating it to the economic instance and systems of interests. This ensures, one is lead to regard these problems of little importance. For Foucault power does not simply takes on a massive form, even if it did, it would still require micropolitical channels to disseminate it throughout the whole of the social body.

If we carefully go through the power theory of Foucault we would immediately find that he is against Marxism. He considers power to be a negative concept. It prevents the political opposition, class consciousness and free expression of impulses. Power is often manifest in frustrated form. On the positive side, however, he considers power as a productive and creative force. Power creates knowledge, methods and techniques. Foucault has analysed all this in his article on *The History of Sexuality.* He says that women should be given power keeping in view of its different dimension. His approach to power is given below:

1. Power is not a thing, an entity, property, quality or commodity. Foucault's this proposition challenges the most prevalent views of power shared by Marxism and Liberalism.
2. He looks at power as something that some individuals, groups or classes have, and wield over who lack it.

Notes and References

1. Beteille, Andre, 'Empowerment', *Economic and Political Weekly,* March 6-13, 1999, p. 590.
2. Hoy, Dewid Couzens, *Foucault: A Critical Reader,* Bessil Blackwell, 1992.

3. Beteille, Andre, *op. cit.*, p. 595.
4. Crook Stephen and others, *Post-Modernisation*, Sage Publications Ltd., London, 1993, p. 125.
5. Causel, Lewis, 'The Notion of Power: Theoretical Developments' in *Sociologic Theory* (4th Edition), Lewis Couser and Bernard Rosenberg (ed.) MacMillan Publishing Co., New York, 1976, p. 152.
6. Eriksen, T.H., *Small Places, Large Issues*, Pluto Press, London, 1995, p. 112.
7. Saneja, Gurew, *Feminist Knowledge: Critiques and Construct* (ed.), Routledge, 1990, p. 59.
8. *Ibid.*, p. 50.
9. *Ibid.*, p. 26.

CHAPTER 2

Tribal Women: The Gender Issue

In all societies there are differences in power between persons. There is not a single society where all adults have exactly the same influence over every decision, where every one have the same rights and duties. Social differentiation and equality are, in other words, universal phenomenon. Gender problem thus today has become a common problem all over the world. However the form and extent of gender problem varies from one society to another. For instance in India we have two broader societies; the caste society and the tribal society. The gender issues in both these societies are found at different levels. The caste society is highly hierarchical. In this society the women suffer from rape, dowry, crime against women, political violence and other such discrimination against women. In the tribal society the gender problem assumes different dimension. In this society women work hard in comparison to men, they are vulnerable to male chauvinism. They are beaten and treated badly. What is worse with the tribal women is that they work all through their life on land, and have no right in the entitlement of land. In the present chapter we look at the gender issues of tribal women *vis-a-vis* non-tribal women in the context of empowerment. Such an approach to the status of tribal women, it would be possible for us to ascertain as to what extent empowerment has helped them. In other words, we look at the tribal women in terms of their discrimination against men.

Gender Issues

Gender has now become a fashionable term to designate the problems related to feminism. In the earlier chapter we have tried to bring about the meaning of gender. We only want to reiterate here that despite the certain biological differences between men and women, women bear certain social and cultural disabilities.

The women all over the world are fighting against this differentiation. The history of this fight for equality goes back to several decades. There have been certain historical forces which have given rise to women's struggle against their subordination. It goes to the middle of twentieth century when there was defeat of fascism, when during twentieth century there was forced retreat of imperialism. These historical forces and particularly the French Revolution of 1789 created a favourable atmosphere for liberty, equality and fraternity.

After the First World War, there was the charter of human rights. This charter among other things bestowed, equal rights to women on par with men. There was a favourable situation for women to fight for their rights. On the other hand, the international development such as the declaration of the International Women's Decade (1975-1985) was a forceful factor to stress for feminism all over the world. During this period modernisation and in European countries post-modernisation had arrived. The new international economic order also created a favourable situation for removing the gender differences. The census operations in Third World countries did not include the work done by women towards the gross national income. There was a faulty definition of work in these censuses. All this underwent tremendous transformation.

The gender problem as we see in India draws heavily from the world women situations. Indu Agnihotri and Vina Majumdar have argued that the international developments have forcefully influenced the women movement in India from the start. They have brought about the parameters within which the movement developed in recent years. According to them the parameters of women movement in India include the following:[1]

(a) the decadal thrust provided by the reparations for the UN Conference in Mexico and the initiatives coming-forth from the Non-Aligned Movement in this context;

(b) the history of and relationship between earlier movements for freedom, equality and democracy values which were subsequently enshrined as basic political tenets in the Constitution of India;

(c) the influence of ideas coming across through the various streams of women's liberation of the West. Thus equality, democracy and freedom were at the same time, actual,

notional and ideological goals which the women's movement addressed in all these connotations including specific gender perspectives and components.

The Indian Movement

Yogendra Singh has argued that social sciences in India have resulted from a large number of social forces in India. The first social force was colonialism and in the princely states, feudalism. Both these forces suppressed the masses of people. In rural India poorer people were made victims of several injustices and discriminations. The sufferings of women were many times greater than the sufferings of men. The women on the one hand, were victimised by the colonial and feudal rule and on the other hand, by their menfolk. Sometimes the victimisation of women by men was far greater than the victimisation of feudal state. Those who are familiar with the Hindi fiction writing would easily understand that the men missed no opportunity to beat the women. Prem Chand, the Hindi fiction writer more than often refers in his novels about the severe beating meted out to women. Hori, the hero of *Godan* whenever gets enraged over the *Zamindar,* he takes recourse to a severe beating of his wife. A survey of Hindi, Bengali and Gujarati fiction writing would immediately show that in rural India women are always discriminated against men. What is worse, even today they are victims of the brutalities of men over women. Arundhati Roy in her Booker Prize awarded novel, *The God of the Small Things,* gives narrations about the men beating women in a drunken state of mind. Thus according to Yogendra Singh colonialism and feudalism contributed much towards the making of social sciences in India.

According to him another social force which gave rise to movements in India was the struggle for Independence. The freedom movement provided ample opportunities to come out openly against the British Raj and princely rulers. Gandhiji openly pleaded for the development of women. This had greater impact on the women's movement. The third force which influenced the gender issues in our country goes to the declarations made by internationalisation of the cause of women. This also includes the whole history for the rights of women. For instance, the Indian National Congress passed the resolution in 1931 for the fundamental rights of freedom, justice, dignity and equality for women as essential prerequisites for national building. This historical force was further strengthened by the Constitution which argued that state would not discriminate women against caste, creed and sex. Thus when we look at the women's movement in India we shall have to look back at the whole historical forces. To refer to Indu Agnihotri and Vina Majumdar again we would say that the women's movement has gone into several forces. These authors assess the importance of these forces as under:[2]

> In contemporary India the resurgence of the women's movement and its contours have to be seen in the light of: (1) The crisis of state and government in the 1970s going into the emergency; (2) the post-emergency upsurge in favour of civil rights; (3) the mushrooming of women's organisations in the early 1980s and the arrival of women's issue on the agenda; (4) the mid-1980s marked by a fundamentalist advance; and (5) the 1990s when the crisis have deepened with regard to state, government and society.

What Agnihotri and Mazumdar argue is that the women's movement as we find today is the result of several political, educational and cultural forces. The women's movement makes efforts at reassertion of citizen's claims to participate as equals in the political and development process. This places the movement in a situation of direct confrontation with the forces of conservation and reaction. 'The fundamentalist onslaught in one country after another have exposed the vulnerability of women's advance in most places. In the Third World as well as erstwhile socialist states, however, the combination of these with the acceleration of free market capitalism has both strengthened the powers of the oppressors, as well as created new instruments for hegemony, by weakening the balancing mechanisms and ideologies that sought to place limits on their capacity.'

In India during the middle of eighties the women were put between tradition and modernity. There have been efforts by traditional forces to keep the women restricted to home. This kind of traditionalism was challenged due to the spread of education and acceleration of modernisation. The change of wind is not restricted to urban India only. It has gone also to villages.

Gender Issues: Caste and Tribal Society

We have in the beginning mentioned that the gender issues in tribal societies are basically different from caste society. As a matter of fact the nature of caste society is hierarchical. It is dominated by considerations of patriarchy and male dominance. The tribal society, on the other hand, is basically an equalitarian society. In this society there is not much marked division of labour. Whatever division the society has is characterised by consideration of age. For instance, a Bhil male would fetch water from the stream and the female would bring fuel from the forest. The male would not hesitate to sit on the grinding mill and ask his wife to clean the cattle shed. The observations of tribal society vividly make it clear that there is not much marked division of labour based on gender. The nature of tribal and caste societies, therefore, give differential nature to gender issues.

In the tribal society there is no problem of dowry. Instead, they have bride price a system. A male gets his wife in lieu of the wealth paid by him to the parents of wife. This is an exchange marriage in consideration of bride price. Second, a marriage among the Bhils is not a sacrament, it is desolate. Divorce is very simple among the tribals. If a wife gets fancy for another husband, the other husband has only to pay the bride price, originally paid by the first husband, to legitimise the divorce. In the caste society the status of women as a widow further creates gender problems. Some one has to look after her family in the state of widowhood. She has to struggle for entitlement in succession in the Hindu family. No such problems of succession arise in the tribal society. As a matter of fact widowhood is no problem among tribals. It would not be wrong to say that widows are exception in this society. Soon after the death of husband, the wife enters into alliance with another husband and therefore she does not remain widow. Only in the advanced age when the old wife does not find an old husband, she remains a widow. The problems related to gender in the tribal society, therefore, different among the tribals.

Traditionalism in Hindu society is a great force. A woman, at least theoretically has a value of virginity. She has to be as chaste as fire. Any premarital or extramarital relations of women are looked with condemnation. A little suspicion can render the life of Hindu women to hell. No such virginity values are upheld by tribal society. It does not mean that the tribal women are promiscuous. They have their contractual relations with the life partner. Any breach in the contract is looked with disfavour. But it does not give rise to gender problems.

The family structure among the Hindus and the tribals is also different. In a Hindu society there is male domination. Women are inferior in the family. The birth of a son gives a salvation to the parents by the offering of oblations—*Pind*. No such values are attached to the birth of a son in a tribal family. True, the birth of a son is a welcome addition to a tribal family. But he does not provide any assurance for salvation. On the other hand, the birth of a daughter in a tribal family is an occasion of joy. When she grows up and is married she brings bride wealth. More the birth of daughters in a family more there is pumping of money in the tribal family.

What we argue is that the gender problem is rooted in the very nature of a society.

Factors Contributing to Women's Studies

Perhaps the recent context of emphasis of women and gender issues go back to 1975—the UN Declaration of Women's Decade. A number of women's studies have come after that. But before this renewal of women's movement there was a long slumber in the field of women's movement after the First World War. The present enquiry is basically concerned with the tribal women's empowerment in the post-Seventy-Third Constitutional Amendment. But the current status of tribal women can hardly be comprehended without taking into consideration the holistic situation of tribal women *vis-a-vis* the women in general.

It is heartening to note that nothing substantial has been done by social anthropologists and political scientists on the gender relations of tribals. The social anthropologist's have an obsession with the tribal studies. They make functional and holistic studies of tribal life. Interestingly enough they have altogether neglected the discrimination meted out to tribal women. We have enough data to substantiate our stand to the effect that the tribal women not only work more than their tribal counterparts, they also work harder than the non-tribal women. To quote a recent study by an economist, B.L. Mehta [3] who says that "We advance the hypothesis that districts with higher proportion of the scheduled tribes exhibit higher FPR mean (average) as well as total." Other sources could also be supported to make our statement that the tribal women work hard compare to non-tribal women. Despite the high achievement of tribal women the anthropologists have not made any academic space for this group of people. Their interest has always been to portray them as bearing tattoos and putting on strange ornaments. They are described as a group of people living an exotic life.

Political scientists have made certain studies into the domain of tribal life. But as tradition would go political scientists more than often cling to voting behaviour and tribal election analysis. The field of tribal empowerment, therefore, is a novice venture for both these tribe of social scientists. It is in this context that we discuss the emergence of women studies in India.

Women's studies have a great importance in understanding the emergence of new gender relations not only among tribals but the women in general. These studies provide theoretical basis for the movement on feminism. These studies also help us to understand the socio-cultural context for gender politics. The new momentum which feminism has taken in post-1975 period helps us to dwell on dynamism which is propelled by globalisation. Actually the women studies which have cropped up during the last more than one decade provide a rich data relating to male domination, power relations, social cultural process which underline the subordination of women. As a matter of fact these studies not only decry the inferiorisation of women in the society, the studies also provide an alternative paradigm for reconstructing the women's life.

However, it must be admitted that some women anthropologists have done good work in the field of tribal women. Among these may be included Iravati Karve, Leela Dube, Tiplut and Nongbri. Nongbri has taken for her study the status of Khasee women of Assam. In fact Nongbri provides data to prove that the Khasee women who live in matriarchal society enjoyed equal gender-relations. But recently with the new succession law and the availability of services in other parts of the country and also abroad, find their women subordinated by men. Besides Nongbri no other social anthropologist to our knowledge has done anything substantial for tribal women. They have not only left out the theme of empowerment, women in general in terms of their discrimination have been left out.

When we come to the discussion of factors contributing to women's studies we find that it was only after the initiative taken by Indian Council of Social Science Research—the apex Social Science Research body of the country, that a very large number of women studies have been carried out. The ICSSR establish a women cell within its outfit and sponsored a large number of studies on women during the period 1976-1980. Beside these studies, a number of workshops have been sponsored by ICSSR.

In the year 1974 the Indian branch of UN published the regional report of the committee on the status of women in India. The regional conference on women's studies and social sciences in Asia endorsed the idea of women's studies. What is important is that the University Grants Commission (UGC) itself provided certain guidelines to its affiliated universities for establishing women cells all over the country. It is believed that the women cells in regional universities would bring out local women problems and not only conduct research but also work as catalyst agent.

An attempt can be made to pinpoint the importance of the women studies for giving a momentum to feminism in India. It must be observed that the nature of women's studies is not unidisciplinary. Actually it is multidisciplinary. In other words, women studies have to explore gender relations not only from political, economic, social, cultural but from the points of view of different disciplines. It is interesting to mention here about the linguistic aspects of gender relations. In a passing reference we would refer to the work of Mahashveta Devi who was awarded 'Gyan Peeth Award'. These days Mahashveta Devi has been working with the denotified classes of nomadic people. In one of her stories Mahashveta Devi gives a version of Dropadi named Dopadi. This Dopadi in the story is summoned by a *Senapati* — through his followers. When Dopadi accompanying the warriors reaches the *Senapati,* she strips off her cloths. Standing stark naked, she stares at him and pushes him with her breasts. The *Senapati* is terrified. Dopadi asked a question: 'can you clothe me'? The *Senapati* could not do anything and had to run away. On the other hand, the Dropadi of the Epic Mahabharat had to request Krishna to give her an endless length of *Sari* to protect her chastity. There is much difference in the tribal Dopadi and caste Hindu

Dropadi. The male discrimination could be countered by tribal women, in such boldness; and this is the message given by Mahashveta Devi.

An Analysis of women studies bring out the fact that the grass-root women are vibrant with power. They give the message of power, the ideology of equality and justice in society. Kumud Sharma[4] in her article on women's studies summarises the three distinct objectives of these studies:

1. to generate and analyse data to uncover socio- economic trends which effect women's situations and to work towards bringing about policy changes;
2. to persuade the social science community to re-examine the theoretical approaches, methodology, concepts and analytical tools which have neglected or excluded women's contribution to society; and
3. to revive the social debate on the women's question which emerged during the freedom movement but faded out during the post-independent period.

The women's studies thus very clearly addressed themselves to policy-makers, the academic community and the general public. 'The programme put an emphasis on research that focussed on women in the poorer and less visible sections of our society—who remain invisible to scholars, planners and policy-makers. It succeeded in generating policy debates on women and development issues and promoted research in hitherto neglected areas such as women's movement, women migrant labour, rural women and women in the informal sector. Its impact on the university system, however, has been marginalised. Within the university system women study is still in the embryonic stage and not necessarily based on reconstructive knowledge from women's perspectives experiences.'

Despite the impressive growth of research women study is faced with several dilemmas both within academic circles and outside. The educational system suffers from many confusions and structural rigidities which creates obstacles in the development of women's studies as an integral part of educational process. Some scholars claim that women's studies is a new discipline which is different from the traditional disciplines of social science in perception methodology, tools of data collection and content.[5] Others refuse to recognise it in this light and argue that women's studies should be incorporated in different disciplines.[6]

People of India Project: The Tribal Situation

According to 1991 census the tribal population in India accounts 12.42 per cent to the total general population. In the state of Rajasthan the tribals constitute 8.10 per cent of the total population. As a matter of fact the tribals have a numerical strength in western India. Besides other tribal groups the Bhils are in larger numbers. They have been residing in the boarders of the inter-states. For instance the boarders of Madhya Pradesh, Rajasthan and Gujarat along with the boarder of Maharashtra, the Bhils have a population predominance.

K.S. Singh of Anthropological Survey of India worked on a major project known as People of India (POI). The project was brought to ground on 2 October 1985. The objective of the project was to 'generate a brief descriptive anthropological profile of all the communities of India, the impact on them of change and development processes and links that bring them together'. According to POI the total number of tribal communities in India is about 461, of which about 172 are segment. The total number of the tribes, their groups and segments including territorial units is 635 which forms the basis of percentage given by the project.

The tribals are spread all over the states except Punjab and Haryana and over all the Union Territories except Chandigarh, Delhi and Pondicherry. Out of their total population in the country, 193.80 per cent are returned from the rural areas, whereas only 6.20 per cent are urbanised. The largest concentration is in Madhya Pradesh (23.22 per cent), followed by Orissa (11.46 per cent), Bihar (11.26 per cent), Maharashtra (11.18 per cent), Gujarat (9.39 per cent), Rajasthan (8. 10 per cent), Andhra Pradesh (6.15 per cent) and West Bengal (5.95 per cent). The smallest population is returned from Goa, Lakshadweep (0.07 per cent), Sikkim (0.14 per cent), Dadra and Nagar Haveli (0.16 per cent) among others.

It is important to look at the size of the tribal populations. The largest tribes are the Goand, the Bhils, the Santhals, the Mina and the Oraon. The tribal people in India inhabit all climatic zones.

However, about 52.4 per cent of them live in areas of moderate climate and 33.5 per cent in areas of warm and temperate climate. They also live in extreme warm climate. About 63.4 per cent of the tribal communities live in hills and forests. The tribal people tend to distinguish themselves by some peculiarity in their dress, for males in 151 communities (23.7 per cent) and for females in 192 tribes (30.2 per cent). The peculiarity consist in headgears including turbans, ornaments, body marking, tattooing a flag or an emblem.

POI has also mentioned some of the bio-anthropological specificities of the tribals. The tribes in India are derived from all four racial stocks, the Negroid, the Proto-Australoid, the Mongoloid, and the Caucasoid. B.S. Guha identified bio- anthropological types among the aboriginals of India:

1. short, with a long and moderately high head, a short and broad face,
2. a dark pigmy strain, with spirally curled hair,
3. the Brachych Mongoloid type, with a short stature and a short feet nose, and
4. a second Mongoloid strain characterised by a medium stature, a longish head and a medium-size nose.

To understand the power position of these tribals it is interesting to find out the social and cultural make-up of the people. The recent studies which have come from French structurologists namely Foucault, Pierre Bordeau, and Habermas show that language is a great source of power. Derrida has developed the concept of discourse. The discourse analysis of most of the post- modernists indicate that language is the source of power. This power is retained by accumulating information. Thus power is held by language and information. It is with this perspective that we look at the language and the dialect situations of the tribes of India. The census of India gives the statistics regarding the language as spoken by the people. Most of the tribals speak Indo-Aryan languages. The second language family is Dravidian and Tibeto-Burman. The POI data show that the tribal communities speaking Indo-Aryan languages are 163, Dravidian 170, Tibeto-Burman 143. Those who speak Austro-Asiatic and Andamanese is negligible. What is interesting is that according to K.S. Singh the incidence of bilingualism, even trilingualism among the tribal communities is far more pervasive than generally believed. All communities except three are non-vegetarian. They eat pork, beef of cow, buffalo and ox. The three vegetarian communities are the Toda, the Rabbaries and Bharwad. It is interesting to observe that all three communities are pastoral. Data on food and diet show that vegetarianism in India both in its historical dimension and in its regional variations is specific. For instance vegetarianism in India has so far been associated with Jainism and Vaishnavism which witnessed the transformation of a pastoral God, Krishna into an incarnation of the supreme God—Brahma. It is interesting to point out here that the pastoral communities which were involved in the growth and development of Vaishnavism were all vegetarians like the Jats, Ahirs etc. The survival vegetarianism among the tribes, therefore, shows the strength of the pastoral traditions in communities which have adopted vegetarianism.

The Bhils of western India and for that matter of south Rajasthan are traditionally non-vegetarians. They were totally meat eaters when they remained restricted to hills and forests. About a hundred years ago they took to settled agriculture. This brought them in close contact with the agricultural castes of the plane, the Brahmins, Patels and other such castes. This brought a Bhagat movement, a variation of Hinduisation among the tribals. The Bhagat Movement which has a sway among the Bhils has spread vegetarian diet. Thus the entry of vegetarianism among the Bhils is not through pastoral life but through agricultural. Today in the whole of western India the Bhils have been influenced by Bhagat Movement, and the variant of Bhagatism found in this part of the country is influenced by Vaishnavism. Besides Bhils, the Santhals, Oraons, Goands and Kawards have also taken to vegetarianism.

Those who are vegetarians take to consume rice, and various millets such as maize and wheat. Wheat has recently been introduced among the people. The tribals unusually use animal fat as cooking medium. The use of oil seeds groundnut, mustard is a new phenomenon. Except for the Bhagats all the tribal men and a considerable number of women in tribal communities consume alcoholic drinks which are generally home-made. They are however, now becoming increasingly dependent on the market for alcoholic drinks.

Are Tribals Hindus?

Long back when V.N. Majumdar wrote about the tribals of India he described them as people having believe in animism. They had a belief in supernatural power. This supernatural power finds its manifestation both in animate and inanimate things. Later in 1951 Census the religion of the tribes was termed as tribal religion. The census enumerators being high caste Hindus, invariably mentioned the tribal religion as Hindu religion. This gave a new twist to the religion of the tribes. With the coming of the conservative political parties in power the debate came into existence by the statement that the tribals are Hindus. Such an observation runs counter to the academic persuasions. We do not have empirical evidence which suggest that the tribals are Hindus—ethnically, racially and bio-anthropologically. It is interesting at this stage of our discussion to refer to the findings of the People of India Project.

K.S. Singh in POI observes that the tribes have generally remained outside the *Varna* system. Therefore, only 11.87 per cent of them recognised their place in it. Another 31.6 per cent are only aware of the *Varna* system. Among those who recognise their place in it, nearly 8.3 per cent claim to be Kshatriya, 7.5 per cent Shudra and 0.9 per cent Brahmins. Almost all tribal groups are endogamous. The incidence of inter-community hypergamy and hypogamy has been reported from 10 to 6 tribal communities respectively, located in Central India and other parts. Most of the tribes practice clan axogamy. Traditionally the tribals have been polygamous though the recent shift is towards monogamy.

To refer back to tribal religion the POI has divided data on religion in two parts. The first part deals with the tribe who follow only one religion. For instance, Hinduism (59.4 per cent), Christianity (23.4 per cent), Islam (3 per cent), Buddhism (6.9 per cent), tribal religion (49.5 per cent). However, many tribes follow more than one religion such as Hinduism and tribal religion (21 per cent), Christianity and tribal religion (13 per cent), and the rest Hinduism, Islam and Christianity. An analysis of trends in tribal religion from 1961 onwards shows that there are three trends: first, there has been a remarkable spread of Christianity among the tribes in north-east India. Christianity has also penetrated in Arunachal Pradesh (4.25 per cent). There has also been a rise in the number of tribal followers of the Christianity in Bihar, Kerala and

Tripura. Elsewhere, in Central India the number of Christians have by and large remained stable. Second, there has been a revival of the tribes on traditional religion. The most significant manifestation has been in Arunachal Pradesh where Donyi Polo—their traditional religion is taken over by Christianity. Thirdly, there has been spread of Hinduism in two forms, the first is the amorphous kind of Hinduism at the local level where both the tribal and folk forms blend, interact and integrate. Ṣecondly, the Santhal form of Hinduism propagated by religious institutions.

The empirical situation of tribal religion that we find today is much confusing. There is evidence to show that the tribals have taken to Hindu Gods and Goddesses. They worship Rama and Krishna, Kali and Durga. They have also taken to Hindu festivals and fast. This suggests the fundamentalists to say that a vast majority of tribals have embraced Hinduism. In other words, tribals have become Hindus. The missionaries assert that the tribals have become Christians. The reality is that despite being tribals Hindus and Christians, they practice in a large number of their traditional animism. 'Jesus' or 'Rama' are alright for them. But they also worship their ancestors and local village deity or hill and forest deity. Thus basically, they are animists though marginally they are Hindus and Christians also. Concluding the findings of POI K.S. Singh very rightly observes:[8]

> A major finding in terms of religion has been the continuance of the autonomy of the tribal religious system. In spite of the tribes' close interaction with Christianity, the hierarchy of the clan and village deities is intact. There are more sacred deities among the tribals from their own communities. The calendar of festivals and festivities is also relatively intact.

Though the tribals continue to profess the core of animism and ancestor worship, they have been gradually drawn into Hinduism. There are a large number of forces influential in tribal belt which influence the tribal people. Historically, the Brahmins have been the model of imitation for the tribals. But during medieval period the Hindu Rajas or chieftains encouraged Hindu religious activities among the tribals. The processes of Hinduisation speeded up more after the introduction of colonial rule in the tribal region. The colonial rule introduced certain rules and regulations which increased certain interactions between tribals and non-tribals. K.S. Singh[9] observes that the process of Hinduisation among the tribals after the nineteenth century through the new Bhakti movements. The objective of this movement as Singh argues has been to counter the Christian influence on the tribals. Most sects are trying to purify the tribals in line with the caste Hindu values. We may refer to a large number of Hindu influences which try to draw the tribals within Hindu fold. On the other hand, the Christian missionaries through the opening of dispensaries, schools, hostels and liberal charitable subsidies have been converting the tribals to Christianity. There have been an agitation among the conservative sections of Hindus against the conversion of tribals to Christianity.

It should be mentioned here that the tribals are not silent over such a kind of religion-oriented cultural transformation. In a national seminar held at Shimla in 1966[10] a Naga participant asked a question "What do you want to make us? Christian, Hindu or Buddhists"? As a matter of fact the tribals are not left to their own decisions. Cultural norms of the dominant groups are imposed upon them. Whatever may be the measure of influence the empirical reality today is that the tribals basically survive today as an autonomous cultural entity. But in this course of discussion nothing worthwhile has come about regarding the status of women. What is the cultural position of gender? The question is important but we do not get any satisfactory historical or ethnographical answer to it. We find that the tribal women follow their men in the field of influence on religion. If, for instance, animism permits women to be non-vegetarian and consumer of liquor, the women too eat meat and drink liquor. If the man becomes a Bhagat, so does the woman. The women do not have their distinct identity. In all cases they identify themselves with the men. There are Bhagatman but no mention is made about Bhagat woman. In animism, there are Bhoopas—the priests who are held in higher esteem. But no tribal women is ever found as priest or Bhupa.

What is worse about tribal women is that in addition to their subordinate or inferior status to men in all fields of tribal life, they have to bear a stigma which is unprecedented in tribal social history. We get rich material on witch hunting among the tribals. Witch is one who has certain magic powers or supernatural powers which help her to inflict injury on a victim which she herself chooses. To possess the distinctive power of supernatural, the woman has to perform certain magical acts. On the fourteenth day of Hindu month in darker nights—*Amavasya,* the woman is required to go to cremation ground in the middle of the night. She has to control the supernatural power on this occasion. She makes sacrifice of her and offers a variety of other things of worship. The power of supernatural, it is said, is of various kinds. One of the power is for inflicting an injury which gradually but surely adversly affects the health of the victim. This power is called *galatveer*—that is the power to melt the health of the inflicted persons. There are various *virs* that is powers of supernatural which are mastered by the practising woman in the art of witchcraft. Such a woman is known as witch —a *Dakan* as she is called among tribals of western India. It is alleged that a *Dakan* can annihilate any person whom she chooses to be her victim. No evidence is required to prove a woman to be *Dakan.* It is the voice of the dominant sections of tribal society or the influential persons who alleged a woman for being a *Dakan.* She is made responsible for certain ills in a man or a woman. If the *Dakan* fails to prove her innocence she is killed manually. The test of proving the innocence is very serious. For instance the alleged witch has to walk on the burning fire, she is required to keep her head deep in water for any length of time. These tests indicate a foregone conclusion—the death of the witch.

The status of women as a witch indicates the gender violence. Social anthropology does not mention much about the status of witch among the tribals but whatever account about witch we get in media is horrifying. She is killed alive then. The history of women is a history of bravery in the tribal accounts. We shall return to it when we discuss the changing gender status among tribals at a later stage. Before we do that we would scientifically examine the status of tribals in Indian society through various stages of history.

Tribal Women in History

Tribal ethnography is very rich in India. The British administrators turned social anthropologists have collected a variety of ethnic graphic data relating to tribals. Risley, Hutton, Russell, O'Malley have given very interesting ethnographic accounts about the tribals. But this kind of British ethnography had an objective to know about the hidden social structure of the people of India. This kind of in-depth data helped the Britishers to consolidate their power in their country. Their another interest was to bring about queer elements of tribal life which depict them as savage, different from the Hindu society. It is because of this that they are described as cannibals — head hunters. They are shown as men of warlike people. This kind of data is very rich in anthropological accounts. Very little is found about the gender relations among the tribals. It is because of the fact that our earlier social scientists did not have any gender perspective. At most they describe the status of women in tribal society. This status was high, equal or low. But the kind of discrimination in gender relations which has become a gender issue in present day society or social science was absent in medieval or modern period. Gender issues as we all know has emerged out of the present feminisation which characterises our present decade. In this section we proposed to look at the gender relations which are found in different periods of history. Wherever possible we will found out historical and ethnic evidences to prove or disprove our observation. In absence of evidence we would only make certain conjunctions.

Dispute and Crisis Regarding the Concept Tribe

The term 'tribe' has become a household word today in India more so the scheduled tribe. Since the suggestions made by B.P. Mandal to the then Prime Minister of India, V.P. Singh, the problem of reservation for scheduled tribes and other members of weaker sections the scheduled tribes has made people to redefine the concept of tribe. There are, theoretically certain issues which require redefinition. Those anthropologists who have worked in South Africa have called the concept quite scandalous. Swartz who has studied the stateless tribes of Africa argues that in political anthropology the concept is used as 'holders.' In other words tribe has become all inclusive concept. But this is only half the trouble. The concept has been criticized on ideological grounds also. In this respect we shall have to look into two societies. One society is that of the people who have a mode of social organisation based on bonds. The tribals are in this respect a dependent mass of people. The second type which we have called earlier a caste society is termed state society by Morris Godlier.[11] These societies are state type societies where there is some kind of a state. Thus there are two societies according to Godlier—the tribal society and the state society. Recently in developing countries also this differentiation has emerged. Godlier brings out the dispute and the crisis of concept of tribe in the following words:[12]

> Now there are many anthropologists and politicians who challenge as theoretically false and politically harmful the use of concept such as 'tribes' and 'tribalism' in order to determine modern contradictions found in underdeveloped countries. They see in the contradiction attributing to tribalism not so much a relic of pre-colonial status. 'Tribal organisation' believed to have been destroyed, but which flower again even violently as a legacy of the colonial period and the new relations involved in new colonial domination.

The disturbance, dispute, and the crisis in concept has not only been found by Morris Godlier, the Marxist anthropologist but also others. Eliot Skinner who has reported about the situation of Upper Volta Republic also mentions such a kind of difficulty with the term:[13]

> It is unfortunate that 'tribalism' with all its connotations of primitivity and traditionalism is the name given for the identity being used by groups competing for power and prestige in contemporary Africa. Some of the names which are now used as symbols for group identities to refer to distinct, socio-cultural entities in the past. However, many of the so-called 'tribal' groups were creations of the colonial period. But even those groups for which continuity with the past could be claimed have lost so many of their traditional characteristics that in fact they must be viewed as a new entities.

The term tribe is also unfavourable to the people themselves. They are called with various names such as *Adivasies, Girijan,* and *Vanvasi.* Gail Omvedt has tried to find out the recent feeling among the tribals of western India. She refers to a conference of Bhil *adivasies* from five states of western India held in a village of Rajasthan. This huge conference of tribals tried to identify themselves as a differentiated group. They made quite clear in this conference their preference for the term *adivasi*. They said that they did not like words like *Girijan* or *Vanvasi*. Omvedt herself argues that scientifically speaking the use of the term 'tribal' for these communities was and is a bit odd. Why? Omvedt explains:[14]

> True there seems to be similarities to historical tribes who had a more egalitarian, clan and community-oriented life-style and culture than agricultural communities under feudalism. But tribes have been communities with economies based on hunting or gathering or simple non-plough agriculture in pre-state societies, occasionally having relations with feudal states, but with mainly an autonomous political economic system. And these have been small societies generally numbering around 30 to 40 in the case of hunting and gathering bands, or in the hundreds in the case of societies practicing early form of agriculture. It was rare to find such known-state societies with numbers in the thousands.

It is quite natural for Gail Omvedt to question use of the term tribe for the communities like Bhils, Santhals, Hos, Mounda, Gaans and others whose total population is in the millions—equivalent to the size of many independent countries. However, at the clause of her observation she prefers the term of tribal instead of *Adivasies*. Her argument is that tribal has both a scientific and a common-sense meaning. The common sense meaning is, and was, insulting and demeaning, the tribals were the most supposedly backward of the native people that the Europeans encountered, contrasting with the powerful feudal states in India and China. Politically the tribals of India were the sections of the population that could be easily romanticised in contrast to the hierarchical Brahminised caste communities of the villages of the plains. Properly speaking, the term tribal when scientifically used, refers to a stage in socio-historical development: use of it for a contemporary community implies that its existence is bound up with that stage, that they will be forever backward.

Scholars like Gail Omvedt have in India expressed their doubts about the use of tribals. The debate though has not taken a serious form in India there are evidences which suggest that we should rethink to review the whole concept which is in a state of crisis. Morris Godlier very rightly observes:[15]

> the concept 'tribe', therefore is 'in crisis'; and there is an urgent need, both theoretically and practically to get to the root of the evil and redefine it in order to criticise and evaluate its real significance.

But the situation becomes a little more troublesome in India. The tribes according to our Constitution are classified as scheduled tribes. In other words the tribes included in the schedule of the President of India are called the scheduled tribes. These scheduled groups were given protective discrimination, in the beginning for ten years starting from promulgation of Constitution in 1950. The discrimination was for a period of ten years. As at present Lok Sabha has extended the period of reservation for the coming ten years that is for 2010. It was believed that the protective discrimination would bring the subaltern tribes on par with the other groups and thus the gap or the hiatus between the tribals and non-tribals would be breached. But this has not happened. And what is worse the more or less egalitarian or homogenous structure of tribal society has developed schism. In other words in the process of directed social change, the tribal society has witnessed striking stratification. They have got divided ethnically and economically. The new social formations that we find among them are on the basis of class system. The elite and the middle class which have developed among them have broken the age old tribal homogeneity. Among the urban tribals, a kind of class war has started. The tribal middle classes along with the high classes identify themselves with the non-tribal classes.

In such a situation any move for de-scheduling the tribals creates raised eyebrows among the tribals and the political parties. All the political parties get their election arithmetic puzzle. Thus retaining the *status quo* of the scheduled tribes has now become a political need. In such a situation if we do we do not take an opportunity to deschedule the scheduled tribes at least the concept has to undergo a scientific definition. True, the concept has lost its social and cultural relevance. Its relevance is only for the central and state governments which are obliged to administer development to tribal groups. We argue that notwithstanding the problems of revising the concept we should, however, be clear about its meaning and implications.

Origin of Tribe in Indo-European Continents

The English word 'tribe' is called 'tribu' in French. The English word comes from the Latin 'tribes' or the equivalent Greek 'phule'. The word thus designate Indo-European institutions of great antiquity. From the outside, the terms related to tribe were empirical and therefore, they have taken different meanings in different societies. Despite the variance the terms in a common form designate a particular kind of social and political organisation in all these societies — Indian or American. It is found that when social anthropology studies a tribal group, it dwells on kinship and political organisation. But this internal relationship between kinship and politics has been largely hidden over the centuries. What has happened is that the kinship and political meaning of the term has gone much more transformation during the last hundred years. As a matter of fact the term tribe has a tag of feudalism, pre-industrialisation and pre-capitalism. When the social anthropologists studied the tribal groups of Africa, Australia, or India all these groups were found at different stages of development. They were food gatherers, pastorals, agriculturalist and now in varying professional categories. About a hundred years back when Malinowski, Radcliff-Brown and Evans Pritchered studied Trobrinders, Azende, the tribal groups were at the stage of savagery. Now these groups have taken to modernisation. The Indian tribals who lived in hills and forest have either got out of forest as a result of deforestation and migrated to plains, towns and cities. They have taken to various professions. They have developed envious political scales. In such a situation there is need to rethink about the original meaning of tribe which was taken by the society. We are afraid such an attempt cannot be made before there is descheduling.

Gender Relation in History

If we want to develop a comprehension about the empowerment of tribal women we shall have to go in the contextuality of the tribal society. We have argued in the beginning that empowerment is not political only; we have argued that power is not limited to political decisions or the decisions relating to local government. Our hypothesis is that empowerment should be multi-dimensional. It should be observed in all walks of life in the domain of gender relations. It is with this holistic perspective that we scan the history of gender relations at the national and local level.

Heterogeneous Society

The tribal society like any other society is not homogeneous. There are divisions in tribal society. Even during the medieval periods there were tribal rulers and the masses of tribals. Earlier to that during ancient period the tribals had their bands each having a band leader. The members of the band were required to pay taxes to the leader and the leader on his part gave protection to the band members. We have instances of tribal rulers. For instance in the Chhateesgarh region of Madhya Pradesh there were Gaond Rajas and Gaonds are the numerically largest group in India. There were Bhil rulers in Panchmahals area of Gujarat, there were Bhil rulers, Bania and Dungaria in the former princely states of Banswara and Dungarpur. The Mina ruled over the erstwhile region of Amber. They were defeated by the Kachwa Rajputs of Jaipur. S.H.M. Rizwi who has worked among the Minas of Rajasthan says that often having lost their power and status at the hands of the Rajputs they lived a status of tribe. All such accounts make it clear that the tribals in some parts of Rajasthan, Gujarat and Madhya Pradesh were rulers.

While living in the hilly region the tribals either depended on hunting and game or lived a pastoral and food gatherer status. In such a society the status of women was quite ordinary. All the arduous and risk involving work was done by the male-folk. In this society women were treated softly. They were not required to accompany their men for hunting game. What was expected of them was to safeguard the house and prepare food for the men. At this stage of tribal development the gender relations were not discriminatory. They were on the side of protection to women. About hundred years back the tribals of central India, Bihar and Orissa took to agriculture. This brought the tribals from hills and forest to plains. Some of them who chose to reside in hills and forest took to a forest life. They earned their livelihood from forest produce, forest game and by selling woods. In some valleys they partly took to agriculture. Women were not discriminated against in the hill and forest life. However, it has been reported that in the hilly region there was practice of polyandry. In the Jayantia Hills of Assam even today there is practice of matriarchy. The Khasa women call the shots. Their husbands are occasional visitors and the property in the Khasa matriarchal society goes from mother to daughter. There are instances of matriarchy in Kerala among some of the sections of tribals. It can safely be said that in matriarchal society men are discriminated against women. The position of women is a better one. In this society there are no gender issues.

However, with the coming of settled agriculture there emerged women discrimination. In an agricultural society though women are required to do lighter job, their help is sought in ploughing; they themselves do not plough. They are required to weed the fields and keep a vigil. But in the earlier periods of settled agricultural land was enough with the tribals. In fact, before the coming of British, land was owned by the community itself. It was never a property. With the coming of *Zamindari* system as initiated by the British, land for the first time became a private property. But in the hills and forest the tribals had a traditional ownership of land. Access to land gave rise to larger families. The tribals developed the notions that if they own more than one wife that is, they practice polygamy they will beget more children. This will give them more women hands and hands of children to work in the field. Obviously, the farm produce would multiply. Such a notion made polygamy a popular form of marriage among the tribals. Second, polygamy also restored a new status to the tribals on par with the Rajput castes. Thus polygamy was both economic and political. This reduced the status of women. It created gender discrimination at two levels. At the level of male and female, the male showed his preference for the youngest wife and in some cases the only good looking wife. At the second level there emerged a rivalry among wives that is discrimination in the same sex. We could now with considerable thought and availability of evidence say that gender discrimination emerge among the tribals with the coming of agriculture and the practice of polygamy.

Simultaneous to polygamy there came polyandry among the tribals. It is a type of marriage where the husbands of a woman are more than one. Anthropologically polyandry is a marriage in which a woman can have more than one husband at the same time. It is found among the Todas of Nilgiri hills of Tamil Nadu. In this marriage the status of women is reduced to the lowest level. She has to satisfy the sex needs of all her husbands along with the services of a wife.

Leaving aside the monogamous form of marriage the tribal women have to bear an inferior status in the society. In the polygamous marriage which is found in most of the tribals of India there is system of bride price. It is also called bride wealth. In western India among the Bhils there is wide prevalence of bride price. Anthropologists considered the status of a polygamous woman as that of a property. The parents think that their daughter is a property which can be encashed when she attains marriageable age. Her husband also expresses a strong sense of possessiveness over her. Sometimes, in a day-to-day behaviour she is considered as a person who is purchased as a commodity. It is in this respect that she is asked to perform all kinds of work. And if, he decides to give her divorce, he is required only to pay back the bride price, he paid to her parents. And, on the contrary, if she takes fancy to some other man, what is required in this situation is that the other man is obliged to pay the bride price which her present husband had paid to her. We give here a case study of a Bhil woman who was treated as a commodity:

> Jamuna is the wife of Gautam. She lived with her husband hardly for six months. Gautam ill-treated her. This prompted her to run away with Vaishta who belonged to a neighbouring village. Soon her husband traced her out. Jamuna's case was referred to the traditional Panchas of the concerning villages. The decision given by the Panchas in this case was interesting. Her parents had received Rs. 2,000 from Gautam. In this case, since she hardly served Gautam, her new husband was penalised to pay Rs. 1,500 in lieu of possessing her.

Jamuna's case very clearly shows that the Bhils, where polygamy is practiced, women are treated as a commodity. It is because of this that we say there is property concept regarding women in tribal society. In this connection it may also be mentioned that among the tribals of western India and elsewhere in the country, a women is not required to be chaste as her qualification for marriage. Pre-marital sex relations are common in the tribe. If this kind of sexual relationship is known to the people, it does not disqualify her for marriage. At worse she may get a lesser amount of bride price. Extramarital relations are also not looked with much disfavour. However, if a woman is found indulging in adultery and caught red-handed, her husband might kill her instantaneously. But rumours about adultery go unheeded.

Pre and extramarital sex relations do not much inflict any social stigma on women. But this has made her status awesome. Moriscarstress, a British anthropologist who worked among the Bhils of Kotra bhoomat observed that there is 'restricted promiscuity' among the tribals. This practice on one hand, has lead the tribal women to serious sexually transmitted diseases and on the other hand, lower down her status in the caste Hindu society. What is important is that in the tribal society the women is presumed to be a thing to be consumed sexually without any loss of status.

Laxity in sex is also observed in other fields of life. There is practice of levirate marriage among the tribals. It is a practice of requiring or permitting a man to marry a widow of his brother. Quite like it there is also prevalence of sorrorate marriage. In this form of marriage a younger sister marries the widowed husband of her diseased elder sister. Both these forms of marriage—levirate and sorrorate are good so far the marital status of the woman is concerned, but all this makes a woman a thing of consumption of the menfolk. She does not enjoy the status of a chaste woman. And the end result is infliction of a number of sex related problems. Recently some evidence has come to light which shows that tribal women living in the villages adjoining national highway (N.H. 8)—which links Mumbai to Delhi, indulge in illicit sex relations with the truck drivers plying on this route. This has landed these women to a kind of brothel life. What is important is that the status of women in the non-tribal society is ranked very low. This low ranking is also due to the traditional tribal institutions of dowry and willy-nilly permission to extra sex relations.

Yet another institutional outfit which reduces the status of women is the procedure of selection of life partner. Tribal women are not associated with any aesthetic sense of art, beauty and working on delicate things. When the life partner is chosen, the Bhils do not look to the artistic tastes and hands of the women.

What is required of a bride is her capacity to be able to take up household work. She should be able to fetch water from well or stream. It is also required of her to go to forest, collect fuel and grind corn. The physical or manual working capacity of the women constitute the basis of her selection for marriage. What is called beauty or artistic skills is almost absent in the tribe. This had reduced the women merely to a manual worker.

Women in Agriculture

Historically we had traced the status of women from medieval to British period. The economic transformation of the tribe has been phenomenal. From food gatherers, hunters, they have moved to subsistence economy. Their subsistence economy now has transformed to cash economy. The tribals produce surplus commodities in the field. There is definite role of women in this economic transformation. It is reported that women have proved themselves to be good human resource development. In order to find out the main activities of tribal women we should know the kind of work performed by tribal women. The main activities of tribal women on the basis of their occupation can be broadly categorised in two groups:[16]

1. Workers.
2. Non-workers.

1. Workers

The tribal women work as a labourer or worker to perform certain functions in the following areas:

1. the agricultural production and related operation;
2. traditional or social forestry;
3. weaving and making handicrafts;
4. dairy, piggery and poultry;
5. fishing;
6. khadi and village industries;
7. agro-based social forestry;
8. construction of roads, buildings and minor irrigation channels;

9. fruits and vegetables;
10. mining and quarrying;
11. sericulture;
12. brick kiln and stone cutting;
13. transport, storage and communication;
14. trade and commerce, and other services.

2. *Non-Workers*

Tribal women perform several other activities like cooking, washing, sewing, fishing, dairying, spinning and weaving, making pickles and *pappads* for home use as well as sale, childcare, collection of fuel, fodder and water. But still may not be counted as worker. Their work is not considered economically productive.

In contemporary India tribal women have entered into a variety of jobs and professions. They get the benefit of reservation of seats. We shall have occasion to discuss the new occupational—professional status of tribal women at a later stage. We only want to stress that the gender relations among the tribals have covered a long socio-cultural space in history. It would be observed here that with the development of the tribal society from savage to civilisation, the gender relations have become more and more complicated. In the past the tribal women were not much discriminated against men. The glaring discrimination as we have discussed above is largely in the field of marital relations. It is here that she is considered as a property either owned by the parents or the husband. In other walks of life the discrimination against man was not much striking. Even today it is she who does marketing. It is she who takes smaller parts of her produce to market. It is she who makes the best of shopping. She does not feel shy to entertain herself by consuming liquor in the company of her kinsmen. She freely moves in the weekly markets, laughs and giggles. However, in major decisions of family issues, she is not consulted. If a part of her land is sold or new land is purchased, she is often marginalised. Even in matters of betrothal and marriage, her advise is not taken. She is only informed. It is interesting to find that all over western India the tribal women managed the household affairs. Generally, the men leave their house in the morning to the nearby town, make gossip there and in the evening return home being tipsy. The men are found hard working on occasions of ploughing and harvesting. The rest of the work is the lot of the women. Despite working hard in the field of production, tribal women are sidetracked in social counselling.

TRIBALS: CONSTITUTIONAL STATUS

There is a hiatus in the conception of tribe between social anthropologists and Government of India or the Constitution. The concept of social anthropologists as developed through the ages considers agricultural tribes, peasant communities and backward sections as the content of tribe. In other words, those who are poor, backward, illiterate and hill and forest dwellers are the tribals. But such a conception of tribe is vague and ambiguous. The Government of India wanted to implement certain development programmes which could raise the life style of these people to an appreciable level. Looking to all this the government constituted a panel which identified the tribes as scheduled tribes. According to the Constitution:

> Any tribe or tribal community or part of or group within any tribe or tribal community as are deemed in Article 342 to be scheduled tribes for the purpose of Constitution.

Thus the groups which are in the scheduled list of the President of India is described as scheduled tribes in India. For including tribal groups in the scheduled list, the President may, after consulting with the governor of state by public notification, specify the tribes which would deemed to be scheduled tribes in relations to that state. Some of the criteria for declaring a group as a scheduled tribe are backwardness, exploitation, poverty, illiteracy, and residing in isolation in the interior parts of the hills and forests. The number of scheduled tribes in the year 1950 was 210. Now this number has increased to 461. Out of this large number of tribal groups, there are a few primitive tribal groups also.

The Constitution has made a differentiation in scheduled tribe and primitive tribe. Anthropologists do not make any such distinction. However, for the purpose of Constitution the primitive tribes are those who have not taken to agriculture as their major source of occupation. Basically the primitive groups are hunters, food gatherers or those who take agriculture in a rudimentary way and do not produce for market. For instance, in the state of Rajasthan the Sehrias are only people who constitute the primitive group. They are found in Baran district of Kota. The Sehrias even today reside in the forest and the hilly terrain. They only take one crop a year during wet weather. The government as per its development programmes has special project for primitive people.

Safeguards for Scheduled Tribes

The safeguards provided by the government have the basic objective of assuring the participation of scheduled tribes 'forest measure in the political, economic and cultural life of the nation'. The scheduled tribes have suffered a lot in the field of development and therefore, the safeguards are provided for their upliftment. Initially the safeguards were made for the period of ten years that is upto 1960 from the date of the implementation of the Constitution. It was, however, provided in the Constitution that if the special officer for scheduled castes and scheduled tribes recommended and is duly supported by the Parliament, the period could be extended further. The Constitution provides for the appointment of a Special Officer who has come to be known as Commissioner for Scheduled Castes and Scheduled Tribes. It shall be the duty of the special officer to investigate all matters relating to the safeguards provided for the scheduled castes and scheduled tribes under the Constitution and report to the President upon the working of those safeguards as such intervals as the President may direct, and the President shall cause all such reports to be laid before each House of Parliament. As at present the safeguard are for January 26, 2010.

The safeguards given by the Constitution permit the state to allow protective discrimination so far as the tribals and weaker sections of the society are concerned. Article 46 of the Constitution lays down:

> the state shall promote with special case the educational and economic interest of the weaker sections of the people, and in particular of the scheduled castes and the scheduled tribes, and shall protect them from social injustice and all forms of exploitation.

To help the proper and smooth implementation of the Directive Principles containing in the Article 45 suitable provisions have been made in the Fifth and Sixth Schedules of the Constitution.

Scheduled Area

Under the Fifth Schedule of the Constitution the President is empowered to declare any underdeveloped area having substantial population of the scheduled tribes as a scheduled area. Such areas have been declared in eight states, namely, Andhra Pradesh, Bihar, Gujarat, Madhya Pradesh, Maharashtra, Orissa and Rajasthan. Though the scheduled areas are administered as a part of the state in which they are situated, the Governor is given powers under this Schedule, to prohibit the application of any central or state regulations or direct its modification in its application, to those areas, and

1. form regulations for the peace and good governance of these areas *inter alia* for prohibiting or restricting the transfer of land by or among members of the scheduled tribes,
2. regulating the allotment of land to members of the scheduled tribes, and
3. regulating the carrying on of business as moneylender by persons who lend money to the members of scheduled tribes.

The government of the state having scheduled areas are also required to make periodical reports to the President, regarding the administration of such areas. The Fifth Schedule also provides for the establishment of each state having scheduled areas of a Tribal Advisory Council, to advice on such matters pertaining to the welfare and advancement of the scheduled tribes in the state as may be referred to it by the government of that state. These Councils must consist of not more than twenty members, of whom three-fourth must be the representatives of the scheduled tribes in the Legislative Assembly of the state concerned. Tribal Advisory Council has so far been set up in the states of Andhra Pradesh and Bihar.

The Sixth Schedule of the Constitution deals with the tribal areas of Assam and North-Eastern Region and not in Bihar and therefore, it is not been discussed here.

Reservation in Parliament

Articles 330, 332 and 334 of the Constitution provides for the reservation of seats for scheduled tribes in Lok Sabha and Vidhan Sabhas of various states. In accordance with the Article 164 of the Constitution a Minister for Tribal Welfare is appointed for Bihar, Madhya Pradesh and Orissa. The Minister in-charge of the Tribal Welfare has to look to the interest of tribals and has to promote with special care, the educational and economic interests of the tribals. What is important is mentioned in this connection is that the scheduled tribes are surely backward in their economy, but there are other caste groups also who are below poverty line. Reservation in Parliament is not on the basis of poverty only. *The Scheduled Tribes are socially and educationally backward classes and therefore they have also to be given programmes for development in these areas. Thus the reservation in Parliament is for economic, social and educational development.*

Reservation in Services

There is protection in services also. Article 335 of the Constitution says 'the claims of the members of the scheduled castes and the scheduled tribes should be taken into consideration in the making of appointments to services and post in connection with the affairs of the union of a state'. Article 16 (4) provides that effect can be given to above provision by reserving posts in favour of the scheduled tribes. Accordingly, 5 per cent of vacancies have been reserved for tribals in direct recruitment by examination conducted on All India basis by the Union Public Service Commission. Similarly, reservations have been made in direct proportion to scheduled tribe population to the concerned subject to a minimum of 5 per cent. However, it should be maintained that the reservation that is given to tribal differ from state to state. In some states such as Tamil Nadu and Karnataka the percentage of reservation goes beyond 50. Reservation is the state subject and therefore varies in percentages

Other Consultancy Services

There are a few other concessions given in services to the members of the scheduled tribes. For instance relaxation of maximum age limit prescribed for appointment to the post is reduced to 5 and also there is reduction to the prescribed fee to the extent of one fourth. Besides there are concessions in services where recruitment is made directly. In some cases discretion is allowed to be used by the appointing authorities to select candidates from the scheduled tribes fulfilling a lower standard of suitability, so long as the candidate fulfil the prescribed minimum technical and educational qualifications. In view of this, a fair number of scheduled tribe members is recruited in the government services in various categories ranging from the post of a peon to a District Magistrate or even above. This recruitment gives a kind of empowerment to the scheduled tribes. The impact on women is also visible. Service in government departments makes tribal women economically independent. As a result of it her gender status improves not only in her family and kin group but the wider society.

Welfare of Scheduled Tribes

For the purpose of promoting the welfare of the scheduled tribes in various states, the Consolidated Fund of India gives grants-in-aid as provided in Article 275 of the Constitution. In all the Five Year Plans the tribal areas were given sufficient aid out of this fund. The programmes drawn up in the different Five Year Plans on scheduled tribes include schemes like assistance at all stages of education, freeships, stipends and hostel facilities providing books, stationery grants, mid-day meals, uniforms, grants of scholarships for technical training, land improvement and land reclamation, minor irrigation, supply of improved seeds, manures, implements and bullocks, development of cattle, fisheries, poultry, construction of roads and bridges needed to the connection of inaccessible tribal areas, preventive measures for diseases common to tribal areas, provision of drinking water in different areas, establishment of medical unit, maternity and child welfare centres and many other requirements of life for the all round developments of the tribals.

Under Article 23 of the Constitution, trafficking in human beings and *begar* have been prohibited. Any contravention of this provision has been made an offence punishable by law. Right to freedom has been granted under Article 19 of the Constitution. Article 19 (F) states: 'All citizens have the right to acquire, hold and dispose of property.' Clause 5 of this article has imposed restrictions in the case of the scheduled tribes when they have to dispose of their property. This restriction has considerably stopped the transfer of property from the scheduled tribes to the non-tribals. In Bihar, the Chota Nagpur Tenancy Act has restricted the transfer of land belonging to the tribals to the non-tribals. Similar Tenancy Acts have been passed in all other states where there are scheduled areas.

The President has further been empowered, under Article 338 of the Constitution, to appoint a special officer to investigate all matters relating to the safeguards provided for the scheduled tribes under the Constitution. He has to report to the President about the working of those safeguards at suitable intervals. The Scheduled Tribes Commission submits an annual report to the President of India stating how far the provision of the Constitution on making special safeguards for scheduled castes and scheduled tribes has been in operation in different parts of the country.

Tribal Policy of Government of India

The tribal policy for the status improvement of different scheduled tribe groups has been made keeping in view the discrimination which these people have suffered. It has been a historical experience. Perhaps one of the disqualification of scheduled tribes has been their isolation from the mainline civilization. If untouchability is the major problem of the scheduled castes, isolation has been the central problem of scheduled tribes. They lived in hills and forest for longer period of history. On one hand, they were suppressed and humiliated by the feudals and on the other hand, they were exploited by the high caste Hindus. Within the tribal society itself, there was a hierarchy. Some of the tribal elites were *Jagirdars*. Such a kind of hierarchy among the tribals created a kind of class system among them. Taking into account the historical exploitation and suppression of the tribals, the Constitution framers gave certain protective safeguards and development safeguards to these people. The Seventy-Third Amendment is a series towards this direction. We have argued earlier that the tribals can improve their status, if their participation is sought in the development and administration of their area.

What principles helped the government to frame its tribal policy? The first guide or the cardinal principle is drawn from the Constitution. Second, the situation of tribals was much discussed by eminent sociologists, anthropologists, social scientists and commissions. For instance, by the end of thirties Verrier Elwin propounded the theory of Public Park, by stating that the tribals should be kept isolated from the non-tribal mainstream. If the isolation is not maintained the tribals would be lost in the corrupt and evil world of non-tribals. G.S. Ghurye another sociologist anthropologist of Bombay University vehemently consented the isolation or Public Park theory of V. Elwin. He argued that the tribal problem was an agrarian problem. According to him the tribals were a backward caste Hindus. D.N. Majumdar, advanced the theory of 'selective integration' of the tribals.

He argued that the tribals should not be allowed to accept anything and everything of the civilized world. Only items of civilization which are deemed to be beneficial for the tribals should be allowed entry into the tribal area. All these theories about the integration of tribals make one thing certain that the tribal problem cannot be considered apart from the general Indian problem.

No specific paper has been brought out by Government of India. And therefore, we can make out tribal policy of Government of India on the basis of its policy and development programmes. Such a policy has made explicit in the guidelines for tribal sub-plan areas 1978-83. The Planning Commission in this document has specified the objectives of tribal development:

1. narrowing the gap between the level of development of tribal and other areas, and
2. improving the quality of life of the tribal community.

Besides this statement of policy the five principles of tribal integration declared by J.L. Nehru also tell us about the government policy. These five principles also known as *Panchsheel* are as under:

1. people should develop along the lines of their own genius and we should avoid imposing anything on them. We should try to encourage in every way their own traditional arts and culture;

2. tribal rights in land and forest should be respected;
3. we should try to train and build up a team of our own people to do the work of administration and development;
4. we should not over administer these areas or overwhelm them with a multiplicity of schemes. We should rather work through and not in rivalry to their own social and cultural institutions;
5. we should judge results not by statistics or the amount of money spend but by the quality of human character that is evolved.

Considering the history of the evaluation of government policies towards tribals it must be observed that they have the privilege and right to project their ethnic identity and their primordial tribal attitudes. But at the same time they are required to integrate themselves and participate fully in the main line civilization which consists of democracy, socialism, secularism and scientific ethics. The safeguards are meant to enable them to take maximum benefits from development actions. So that the gap between the average living of the tribal and the non-tribal is bridged and their quality of life improved.

Considering the status of tribals through different stages of historical development it could be said that the tribals have lived in isolation right from ancient Indian history to independence. They have been victims of suppression and exploitation. The status of women in such a historical background has also witnessed changes. We have argued earlier that during the initial period of history the tribal women did not suffer from discrimination. They moved along with the men. But when the tribals took to agriculture, migrated from forest and hills to plains, came in close relationship with the caste Hindus there appeared discrimination of women against men.

For some time in history the tribal institutional outfits supported them against discrimination. The relative absence of widowhood, child marriage, divorce helped the tribal women to safeguards themselves. But the institution of bride price reduced their status to a commodity. On the whole, before the Hindu institutions made inroads in the tribal hinterland, the tribal women enjoyed more or less on equalitarian status. With the introduction of protective and development safeguards, there emerged an improvement in their status. Not only this Seventy-Third Amendment but the development safeguards in the form of education, service migration also empowered them. In the present inquiry we have reiterated that empowerment is not only in democratic institutions. It is comprehensive in its scope. And in this work we shall examine it for a wider perspective.

References

1. Agnihotri, Indu; Mazumdar, Vina, 'Changing Terms of Political Discourse', *Economic and Political Weekly*, July 22, 1995, p. 1869.
2. *Ibid.*, p. 1869.
3. Mehta, B.C., 'Gender and Regional Patterns of Work Participation in Rural Rajasthan', *Manpower Journal*, Vol. XXXV, No. 2, July-September, 1999, p. 23.
4. Sharma, Kumud, 'Women's Studies in India: Academic and Action', *The India-Canada Relationship* (exploring the political, economic and cultural dimensions) G.S. Graval and Hugh Jobston (eds.), Sage, New Delhi, 1994.
5. Report on the proceedings of the *National Workshop on Planning Women's Studies in Indian Universities*, SNDT Women's University, Bombay, 1989.
6. Mazumdar, 'Emergence of Women's Question', Karlekar, Third Survey of Research.
7. Mazumdar, D.N., *Races and Cultures of India*, Kalyani Publishers, New Delhi, 1990 (Reprinted).
8. Singh, K.S., *The Scheduled Tribes*, People of India, National Series, Vol. III, Oxford University Press, Calcutta, 1997.
9. Singh, K.S., Hinduism and Tribal Religion: An Anthropological Perspective, *Man in India*, 1993.
10. Singh, K.S., (ed.), *Tribal Situation in India*, Centre of Advance Study, Shimla, 1964.
11. Godlier, Morris, *Perspectives in Marxist Anthropology*, Cambridge, London, 1978, p. 70.
12. *Ibid.*, p. 71.
13. Skinner, Elliot, 'Group Dynamics in the Politics of Changing Societies: The Problem of Tribal Politics in Africa', Essays on the Problem of Tribe, Proceedings of the *American Ethnological Societies*, 1968, pp. 170-85.
14. Omvedt Gate, 'Unfair Label' *The Hindu*, Sunday, February 13, 2000.
15. Godleir Morris, *op. cit.*, p. 72.
16. Swmawat, G.S., 'Development of Tribal Women as a Part of Human Resource Development', *Tribe*, Vol. 28.

CHAPTER 3

Tribal Sub-Plan Area

According to the Scheduled Castes and Schedules Tribes Orders 'Amendment' Act 1976, there are 59 scheduled castes and 12 scheduled tribes included in the list of President of India. The scheduled tribes include Bhil and its sub-categories. Bhil, Mina, Damor, Dhanka, and its sub-categories, Grasia, Kathoree, Kokna, Koli, Nairka, Patalia and Cehria. Among these twelve scheduled tribe groups, Mina and the Bhil constitute 93.97 per cent of the tribals. The Mina are the first largest group (49.47 per cent) and the Bhil the second group (44.50 per cent) in the state. The remaining about 6 per cent constitute eight tribal groups of the state. It is interesting to note that the Bhils who are the most numerical people in the state have no place as a tribal group in the country. The Mina hardly bear the characteristic of a tribal group. It appears they have assumed the character of a caste group, close to the Rajputs. They do not reside in scattered villages. Neither their habitat is hilly nor it has a forest cover. They do not have polygamy. And above all economically they are far better than the Bhils. Much of their inclusion in the tribal list is because of their political clout. However, we do not want to enter into the controversy of their inclusion in the scheduled tribe category. We only want to stress here that the Bhils are in the real sense a numerically measure group in the state.

According to 1991 census, out of the 44 million population of the state, 12.44 per cent are tribals. They are found in the districts of Banswara, Udaipur, Dungarpur, Chittorgarh and parts of Sirohi. The Central Government has adopted two models of tribal development. The one model of development is called Regional Development Programme. These programmes include all centrally sponsored programmes which relate to the areas of agriculture and allied services. Co-operation, water, power development, transport and communication, social and community services, economic services are also included in the development programmes. The second category of programmes is called individual beneficiary programmes. The former category of programmes are administered through Tribal Sub-Plan Area and the individual beneficiary programme through MADA, that is Modified Area Development Agencies. The objectives of this programme is to help individual tribal families to improve their quality of life and to raise income and wealth.

There is yet another third kind of tribal development programme called Saharia Development Programme. The Saharia are a primitive group. They have very recently taken to agriculture as their main source of income, forest being their secondary occupation. The Saharia are found in the Shahabad and Kishanganj tehsils of Baran.

Tribal Sub-Plan Area (TSPA)

It was during the Fifth Five Year Plan (1974-79) that the idea of Tribal Sub-Plan was brought to ground. In order to streamline more and more need-based and result-oriented programmes—a task force on development of tribal area was set up in 1972 with the following terms of reference:

1. to review the nature and level of development that had taken place in the scheduled area;
2. to suggest a perspective of development for a period of 50 years;
3. to formulate proposals for Fifth Plan indicating priorities, policies, programmes and outlays in the light of the perspectives.

Five working groups were set up under the task force. These working groups observed that tribal areas were primarily linked to the general backwardness of the areas, the poverty of the people and the unfriendly environment of the area. It was realised that the tribal development cannot be carried out effectively without the development of the area. In other words, tribals cannot be considered in isolation of the area which they inhabit. Therefore, the development of the area and the development of the tribals go together. In such a strategy it is possible that some of the benefits of tribals would be shared by the non-tribals. For instance, if the Samiti headquarters are linked with a *pakka* road to the district headquarters, this will benefit the non-tribals also. But the argument came to the consensus that area infrastructure is the prerequisite of tribal development. This was a major decision and the area for Tribal Sub-Plan was identified.

The Tribal Sub-Plan Area consist of the districts of Banswara, Dungarpur, Chittorgarh, seven tehsils of Udaipur district and two tehsils of Sirohi district. The remaining areas where the tribals are residing in different pockets MADA programmes are implemented. Thus the Tribal Sub-Plan Area comprises of 19 tehsils covering 3,844 villages. In the TSP area Bhil, Damor and Mina constitute the three major groups. According to 1991 census, the region consists of 12.9 per cent of the total area, 16.1 per cent of the total population. Some of the socio-cultural characteristics of the TSP area as under:

Illiteracy

The spread of literacy is a post-independent phenomenon. It is because of this that the literacy rate in the area is 18.8 per cent as against 38.2 per cent of the state. The female literacy rate is shocking. It is hardly 3.5 per cent. Interestingly the women literacy rate at the country level is 39.42 per cent and the state level it is 20.84 per cent. And there has been a gap which has increased from the earlier literacy rate of 1981. However, it must be admitted that the literacy rate among the non-tribal groups is on par with the average literacy rate of the state. For the tribals to attain lower literacy rate, their habitation pattern is largely responsible. In the TSP area the Bhils normally do not reside in compact villages. This kind of pattern is only found in the plains. In *Pals* and hilly region the tribals have a scattered pattern. In such villages each house or a cluster of houses is erected on a raised ground or a hillock. One house is separated by surrounding hills from the other houses of the village. The houses are not herded together. In such a pattern of habitation the area of a single village comes around one to fifteen km. The biggest villages may have larger area. In the scattered villages it is difficult for a school to function effectively. If the school building is closer to one house, it is far away from the rest of the houses of the village. To reach the school, a boy or a girl has to walk down a distance of 15-20 kms per day. This makes attending schools difficult and tiresome. For girls it becomes all the more inaccessible. In between the household and the school a *nalla* or a pasture land or a forest cover has to be measured. These are some of the factors which make literacy difficult and still more difficult for women in the tribal region.

Deforestation

Yet another feature of TSP area is the declining trend of forest cover. True some five or six decades back the whole region was rich in forest cover. Writing in the census of 1891 Web observed that the forest between Partapgarh and Banswara was the richest one in the whole of former Rajputana. The district of Udaipur which was also rich in forest has now been ruined in this aspect. The process of deforestation is fast decreasing and this has resulted not only in the loss of forest wood and fuel, it has also deprived the people from minor forest produce. The wild animals which used to be game for the tribals have now mostly disappeared. Initially the tribal economy was forest based. It has now become agriculture based.

Big Dams and Declining Agriculture

True, big dams provide facilities of irrigations. But such dams are not without their after effects. We have enough literature on the disadvantages of big dams. Arundhati Roy in her analysis on the Sardar Sarovar Dam argues that 'big dams started well, but have ended badly, there was a time when everybody loved them, everybody had them—the communists, capitalists, Christians, Muslims, Hindus, Buddhists. There was a time when big dams moved men to poverty. Not any longer. All over the world there is a movement growing against big dams'.[1] Whatever Arundhati Roy says might prove true for TSP area. There are a few big and small dams in this area, the Mahi Bajaj Sagar Dam and the Jakham Dam being the big dams. The Som Kamla Dam and a few others of this kind are more dams. As a result of irrigation facilities from these dams the fertile land of the TSP area has become silent. There is water logging, the farm produce being reduced considerably. Some of the poor tribals who could take some farm produce for their livelihood are deprived of this source. Arundhati Roy has proved right in the case of TSP area when she says: 'ecologically too they are in the doghouse. They lay the earth to waste. They cause floods, water logging, silently, they spread disease. There is mounting evidence that links big dams to earthquake'.[2]

There is yet another special feature of the irrigation facilities from dams in TSP area. What a tragedy of tribals? The catchment area of the dams have deprived thousands of tribals from their homeland—their fields, their wealth, their households and above all their forests. And the irrigation facilities has gone to the peasantry residing in the plains. There is a simple principle of the gravitation of water. It moves from hills to plains and tribals have been living in the hills. In such a situation the larger benefits of irrigation have been cornered for the non-tribal peasantry. We know that we are not writing one essay on the usefulness of dams. We only want to stress here is that in the TSP area the programmes of development have to be analysed in the contextuality of dams and their irrigation benefits. In other words if the tribals have to be helped to generate farm income some irrigation facilities of the kind of well and water shade schemes have to be promoted. In any development programme the regional topography and the environment diversity occupy a priority position.

Occupational Pattern

Admittedly the tribals are late comer to agriculture. Their entry to this occupation hardly goes to about a hundred years. Whatever pattern of agriculture that the tribals have has been learned from the caste Hindus. The Commercial crops such as that of sugarcane, tobacco, groundnut and soyabean that the tribals have began to take is due to the efforts made by the TSP area and the pattidar migrants who have come from Gujarat. The women are participants in agriculture and other household works. It is found that at all India level the work participation rate among the tribals is 43.71 per cent which is 40.63 per cent in Rajasthan and 41.10 per cent in TSP area. It could, therefore, be said that the women participation in TSP area is a little better than the state level.

The tribals in a larger way have taken to agriculture and it is their main occupation. Earlier this occupation provided them subsistence only. It is recently that the tribals have some surpluses in the field which are brought to market. But the problem with the tribal peasantry is that they do not have infrastructural facilities to bring the produce to the local mandies. This makes the commercial agriculture economically a bad bargain. The TSP area is also required to take into consideration the present state of agriculture among the tribals.

Health

We must say that here we are not discussing the development achievements of the TSP area, that we proposed to do at a later stage. Our objective here is only to provide a valid background which would help us to analyse the empowerment of women. In other words, we only want to know how would empowerment affect the life of the people of area. It is in this respect that we have identified some of the areas of tribal life might have received benefits from the experiment of empowerment. The question is: will empowerment promote women to change and restructure the occupational and health situation? This is the perspective which guides our discussion in the present chapter.

Health perhaps is the first priority for any tribal development and for that matter empowerment. Perhaps, it is expected, women empowerment would affect the total family life and gender relations in the tribal society. It has now been realised all over the world that first care of women should be taken in the field of health. The reason behind this newly identified premise is that compared to other countries, female mortality and infant mortality rates of India have far greater scores. These have to be reduced. It means that we shall have to take all steps to safeguard the health of women. The crisis that come in the life of a woman are pregnancy, post-delivery and rehabilitation after delivery. Related to it is the problem of new vital care. Both these crisis can be resolved if proper medical facilities for women are given in the TSP area. Child delivery facilities have to be improved.

Yet another crisis which the women face in the tribal area is the growth of population. Women have to be educated about sex. It is they who have to take decision whether they would like to conceive a child. The experience the country has about arresting the growth of population explosion is the education of women. Kerala shows that if a girl has passed only seventh standard she has an appreciable number of children, never more than two. It shows that much of population growth is related to two basic factors: education of mother and maternity health facilities. If we think in national perspective we shall have to relate women empowerment with health, and education. Any propaganda, any postures regarding two children and happy family would not make any substantial yields if elementary education is not imparted to women. We only want to bring home the fact that tribal health, population and education have not to be dealt with in isolation. They are mutually inclusive.

At this point of our discussion we shall also have to keep in mind that the national policy of health and population run counter to the traditional ideology of the tribals. It has been a forceful notion of the tribal people that larger population is also beneficial for the family. The axiom is simple: more children bring more health. In the past land was available in plenty. Forests were rich in produce. Larger number of children ploughed larger portion of land, larger number of children collected larger number of forest produce. And above all larger number of children bestowed greater status on the head of the family. Add to it, the practice of polygamy; more wives yield more children simultaneously. One more addition to this dimension requires to be made. The model of imitation for the tribals have been the Rajputs in south Rajasthan. Once upon a time, Rajputs were the rulers. So also, once upon a time the tribals were also rulers of the land. If the Rajputs could practice polygamy why not the tribal? Thus the empowerment measures should not be considered only in a restricted sense. If women get political power or powers to decide matters at the Panchayati Raj Institutions, they should also be empowered to create a cultural bias to abandon polygamy and encourage the role of women in deciding matters concerning gender relations.

Excessive Drinking

The tribals are known for their notorious habit of drinking liquor. We do not very doggedly preach for a ban on liquor drinking. Who does not abhor drinking? Even the high caste Hindus for whom liquor was taboo, have taken to drinking. Many of the decisions regarding business management are taken in five star hotels over liquor drinking. It becomes very contradictory that the 'Sanskritised' and 'Westernised' sections of society more and more take to liquor drinking and preach the tribals for abandoning this habit. Liquor drinking is a primordial trait of tribal community. In the past they brew their own liquor out of *Mahua* flowers and took it satisfactorily. But as Werier Elwin reports that home brewing of liquor is not as simple and ordinary as we think. If a tribal brewed liquor he had to take the consent of his wife and mother first. When the liquor was taken, it had to be given to the relatives, who live in the same village and a tribal village is exogamous. Every one is related to everyone. In such a situation, the women of the house make a fair distribution of liquor to the kins people. What is important is that the tribal should be asked to take liquor moderately. And here is the rub. If the women are subjectively given sense of their statutory empowerment they can play an important role in prohibiting liquor from the village. We want to reiterate that empowerment of women is a very comprehensive phenomenon. It has several dimensions and the development catalysts should try to employ it in non-political such as socio-cultural matters also.

Transport and Communication

Women empowerment in a broader way, we argue, revolutionise the traditional gender relations in the tribe. There was a time when the tribals were isolated from the mainline culture. Now this has become a thing of the past. Transport and communication have in a moderate way reached to the doors of tribals. Many of the villages have got electricity. Some of the villages are linked with telephone. The road network has brought the people closer to the mainstream. Actually a few of the villages close to the town and city are getting the shape of a global village. There has been a flood of the emergence of market. A heartening thing for non anthropological social sciences is that the weekly markets which occupied a central place in tribal marketing, are increasingly becoming irrelevant. We have a reports from Tehsils and interior tribal villages that weekly markets are no more held in the tribal areas. How do we explain it? About 50 years back the tribals came to weekly markets for the purchase and sale of commodities. Obviously, there was no market in their village. Now markets have reached the remotest villages and this has made the weekly markets stand in non-existence. Globalisation has added this new feature to village life.

The daily newspapers have one report or the other too inform that television, electronic media, computer, internet have become parts of new technological culture. A few of our politicians and chief ministers are increasingly becoming superman. Looking to the present speed of the spread of information technology, the tribal sub-plan area has to revise and redefine their targets. As a matter of fact we should look at the problem of empowerment with this near future perspective in mind.

Empowerment, Development and Cultural Crisis

Tribal Sub-Plan Area is basically an *administrative area* identified to help the majority of tribals living in the area. And, then tribals have been defined by the Government of India not out of some specific criteria. They are defined in *administrative terms*. So far development targets are concerned the definition of Tribal Sub-Plan Area and the tribe itself goes very well. But the tribals are also carriers of culture. They are cultural entities surviving in an autonomous wave for centuries. As a cultural group they are also a part of the wider cultural region of the state. If we consider the country as a civilizations unit, the state is a part of wider culture. In the state culture there are a large number of sub-cultures which could be termed regional culture.

For the State of Rajasthan there are a few sub-cultural regions such as Dhoondar, Harottee, Bridg, Marwar, Vagar, Mewar and so on. These regions are based on the attributes of ecology, caste cluster, occupations, historical units and above all language and dialects. The tribals of TSP area the only one of the state falls into two cultural sub-regions—Vagar and Mewar. In both these regions there is much difference in language, diet, dress pattern and fairs and festivals. These two regions are culturally diverse but politically and administratively one. The history of the two sub-cultural regions is different. The Wagad region is close to Gujarat on southern and western sides. The eastern part of the region is close to Malwa — a part of Madhya Pradesh. The language Wagadi is influenced by Gujarati and Malwee. On the northern side of Wagad is Mewar. Wagdi, therefore, has also words from Mewar. The region of Wagad thus have evolved from a three-prong impact of Mewar, Gujarat and Malwa.

What we want to argue here is that the gender relations among the tribals result from this three-prong cultural influences. There is lesser of the observation of *Pardah* among women. There are fewer child marriages. Women participate openly in public functions in Wagad. In southern Rajasthan, Dungarpur was the only princely state where women participated openly and boldly in the freedom struggle. The brutalities of feudal rule were faced by women with all their might in the state. The statutes of Nahi Bai and Kuri Bai—the Bhil women installed outside the old city gate show vividly the role played by tribal women in the princely states. The former Mewar does not have any record of tribal women's participation in freedom movement.

Our argument is that when we talk about empowerment of women in the Sub-Plan Area, we should not forget that gender relations in the sub-culture regions of Rajasthan are not homogenous. The Bhil women of Mewar are substantially different from the Bhil women of Dungarpur. And Bhil women of Banswara are lesser developed from Dungarpur. In the field of education also there are differential. During the princely rule there was much awakening about elementary education in Dungarpur. The Bhil Seva Mandal lead by Bhogi Lal Pandya and Gaurishanker Upadhyay made tremendous progress in tribal region. The region of Mewar has a different history. It had been a state where there was a network of Gandhian educational institutions which promoted education among the masses of tribal people. No such educational mission worked in Banswara. Interestingly enough former Banswara state had a network of mission schools, dispensary, hospitals and agricultural centres. These missions were conspicuously absent in Dungarpur. And in the former Mewar state there has been only one Catholic Church at Udaipur with a meagre spread in the villages of Pai and its neighbourhood. Christian missionary work in Mewar never reached in the remote tribal hinterland.

The working of mission in the tribal area has given educational opportunities to the women. In the state of Banswara, if education was not imparted through voluntary agencies, it was spread through Christian missionaries. The point of our discussion is that the gender relations in the whole of TSP area have never been uniformed or homogenous. It has always been varying. Though the area is geographically contiguous, administratively one. The area is different so far discrimination against women is concerned.

What has happened in the TSP area is that the Government and NGOs have been busy to create resources for generation of income. It is believed that if, economic status of the tribal, that is if tribals are brought from substantive level to diversified economy, many of their problems would be solved. It is correct that if proper measures are taken the lifestyles of tribals would experience transformation. In the enthusiasm of improving the status of the tribals hardly any attention is paid to the cultural crisis which the people face. On the other hand there are some fundamental forces which draw the government both at the state and central level in controversy about Christianisation and Hinduisation of tribals. The real problem is not conversion, the tribals are faced with the problem of their cultural identity. What is worse, the leaders of the feminist movement also look at the tribal gender relations from the perspective of high-caste Hindu and the urban way of life. True, the urban women are becoming victims of dowry and inferiorisation of women. True, there is lesser representation of women in parliament. But these are some of the issues which have national importance, the issues are also not without debate. However, in the context of tribal women it must be said that their problems are basically different from urban and high caste women. Deepa Mehta's problem of the plight of widows which they experience at Varanasi or Vrindavan, are never experienced by tribal women. Neither do they suffer from the plight of dowry. Our experience in the field shows that at no time in tribal history, brides are burnt among tribals. Their problem is bride wealth that is bride price. If there is some problem in acquiring a wife, it is the problem of the groom's parents. The role of mother-in-law is almost absent among tribals. The tribal family is quite unlike the Hindu family or the general pattern of family in India. Among the tribals as soon as a boy becomes matured and the parents are in a position to manage the bride price, the boy is married. And soon after marriage he is asked to erect his own house. The daughter-in-law manages her own household chores. She does not come in conflict with the mother-in-law. The traditional daughter-in-law tension and recurring conflicts are absent among the tribal women. The daughter-in-law has never to confront her mother-in-law. *All these indicates that the gender relations among the tribals are so different that they do not constitute the oft used agenda of feminist movement. Our argument is that the gender situation all over the country emerges from a particular society. Discrimination of women against men is variable from one society to another.*

Not only tribals but the nation as a whole is in the grip of cultural crisis. Globalisation, liberalisation and privatisation have affected all the segments of the country. The tribals are no exception to this overall holistic change. Yogendra Singh writes:[3]

> Many visible and significant, cultural changes have taken place in India since independence. Across the nation, the lifestyle and leisure time activities of the people have changed. It includes modes of consumption, style of dress, uses of synthetic materials or artefacts, modes of transport, and the weakening of traditional ingredient about the consumption of vegetables and meat products now have a wider base. The 'green revolution' that took place in 1970s is now supplemented by a 'white revolution'. The evidence proved by the Peoples of India (POI) survey and the National Sample Survey supports the large extent of these changes. Where, on the one hand, ethnic and regional self-consciousness or identity of castes, tribes, minorities or other regional groups is increasing, there is evidence also to support the prevalence of many integrative cultural processes within our society which contribute to the growth of a holistic consciousness. There is increased inter-regional migration which makes it possible for regional, cultural trends, cutlery products, cultural performances, ritual forms, styles of dress and ornamentation to flow to other parts and mix together.

Globalisation, and intermixing of cultural trends within the country have influenced the tribal culture in the greatest possible manner. This is not anything specific to tribals. But the tribal society is also experiencing this new kind of cultural change. The People of India Project (POI) has identified 91 cultural regions within India.[4] In each cultural regions there are several sub-cultural regions. In such a categorisation the tribals constitute a distinct cultural category. The changes which have come have affected the identity of the tribal group. If the tribal identity is lost with the regional identity state or national identity what would happen to the ethnic survival of the group. It is very interesting to ask in this context as to the differential attributes of the tribal *vis-a-vis* the non-tribal women. Young tribal girls have began to visit beauty parlours at the town and city level. They wear *bindi* and *Mehndi*. They tie thin sari on urban pattern. Their verbal conversations are in Hindi. In such a situation it becomes very difficult to distinguish tribal women from non-tribal women. The problem is that of the autonomy of the tribal cultural identity. Yogendra Singh poses the question:[5]

> In the context of overall social change, it is essential to examine the nature of relationships that demands for cultural autonomy or ethnicity have with the processes of cultural integration in the Indian society as a whole. Sociological studies suggest that existence of viable linkage between two otherwise contradictory process. Cultural integration of diverse entities in pan-Indian society has had a long history in India. The Matrix was that of civilization. This civilization was not sub-summed in out acrossed religious, ethnic, linguistic and regional boundaries.

Yogendra Singh's solution to the cultural identity refers to civilization. He argues that each ethnic group would maintain its autonomy but at the same time become a part of the pan-Indian civilization. In other words the tribal society as an ethnic identity is likely to maintain its survival provided other cultures do not impose themselves on them. However, this is not our premise of discussion. We only want to say that the Tribal Sub-Plan area should also look into the continuity of tribal culture while giving empowerment to women.

We have tried to analyse the socio-cultural counters of TSP area of Rajasthan. It is within this wider framework that we would look into the introduction of empowerment of women. Empowerment is never exclusive. It has the character of holism. In the pages that follow we shall discuss women empowerment in its totalisation.

Notes and References

1. Roy, Arundhati, *The Greater Common Good*, India Book Distributors, Bombay, 1999, p. 7.
2. *Ibid.*, p. 7.
3. Singh, Yogendra, 'Significance of Culture in the Understanding of Social Change in Contemporary India,' *Centre for the Study of Social Systems*, JNU, 1994, p. 4.
4. *People of India, op. cit.*
5. Singh, Yogendra, *op. cit.*, p. 6.

CHAPTER 4

Panchayati Raj, Seventy-Third Constitutional Amendment and Empowerment of Women

Despite his charismatic leadership, Gandhiji was deep-rooted at ground level. He elaborated his theory of Panchayati Raj in his *Gramswaraj*. During his times the British Anthropologists were trying to establish India's villages as little 'republic', each village being an autonomous unit. Gandhi and other leaders and intellectuals constituted this kind of idea. True, the villages were autonomous but at the same time they have always been a part of Pan-Indian civilization, nothing short of it. India has always been organic in its structure. When the Constituent Assembly prepared first draft of our Constitution, it was referred to Gandhiji. In anguish, he tore off the draft and said that nothing was acceptable to him without the Panchayati Raj for the villages. It was on his instance that the Constitution made it explicit in the Directive Principles of the State Policy.

The establishment of Panchayati Raj by the state governments is no obligatory gesture to India's more than five lakhs villages. It is the Constitution which has made it obligatory. The idea behind the Panchayati Raj is the decentralisation of power. In a democracy which is participatory at grass-root level, people have to be involved if democracy is meant to be successful. If we recall the history of village development, we would find that the country started with Community Development Programme (CDP) in 1952. The objective of CDP was to make the villages self-reliant. When the self-reliance was attained, it was planned, the CDP would be withdrawn. The ideas and the objectives were carefully made. But the development programmes could not give any self-sufficiency to people. They took these programmes as government imposition, the participation of people being very unhesitating. As a result of it Balwant Rai Mehta Committee, he himself being the Chairman, was constituted. The Committee suggested for decentralisation of power. It argued that development powers should be given to the people at the village level. People should have power to decide their priorities and build their development structure. Mehta's decentralisation prescription later on come to be known as Panchayati Raj. It is heartening to note that Rajasthan was the first state to experiment with the innovation. Rajasthan has been characterised by feudal rule all through its historical periods. If such a state opts for Panchayati Raj, the incidence is un-historical. With the grounding of Panchayati Raj, the Zila Pramukh, Pradhan, Sarpanch and Ward Panch became the unofficial catalyst of development. It created a debate in bureaucratic and political corridors. It came to be known as official *versus* non-officials. However, the bureaucratic circles had to succumb to the dominance of non-officials in the task of development.

The earlier enactment of Panchayati Raj gave proper representation to the tribals. If for instance, in the earlier status of Panchayati Raj members of scheduled castes and scheduled tribes were not elected, they were co-opted for an effective participation. We had experiences of tribal non-officials to run developmental administration. The experiment, however, did not make several success stories. It was reported that the tribal non-officials did not have the skills and education which is required for development. They became victims of corruption and exploited the people in collaboration with the officials. The history of Panchayati Raj as it existed prior to Seventy-Third Constitutional Amendment has not been rosy and optimistic. The Planners were conscious of it. They carried the hope that if women are made effective participants in development it will have two basic advantages. One, theoretically the women would have a statutory position in the task of development administration; second, the empowerment would perhaps give a new momentum to tribal development. As elsewhere, in the present analysis we argue that women empowerment would give a new boost to village development. In this connection, nevertheless we should not forget that the successful running of Panchayati Raj presupposes the skilfulness and education of tribal women. Amartya Sen when said that elementary education was a bed-rock for the development of Third World countries. His argument is meaningful when we look at the literacy background of women in Rajasthan. Women can effectively run Panchayati Raj if they have some elementary education and some sort of administrative experience. One can take a sound position when one understands that administration of development is not gender-oriented. A man would fail miserably so will the woman if, she or he does not have the technical and administrative know-how to perform the development task. These are the few of the prerequisite which need to be taken care of in promulgating the Seventy-Third Constitutional Amendment. The new Amendment has come out of a historical experience. The empowerment given to women in the amendment is not merely a metaphor or a political gimmick. The act has a logical and political argument and has to be understood in this context. In the following section we look to the salient features of the provisions of the Seventy-Third Constitutional Amendment.

Major Features of Seventy-Third Amendment in Terms of Women Empowerment

It was in 1993, during the month of April that Seventy-Third (Constitutional Amendment) Act came into force. And all the States of the Union have amended their laws relating to Local Self-Government. The Act provides one-third of the seats for women out of the total seats. The Act is meaningful because it is for the first time in India's history that women have been given reservation at grass-root level democratic institutions. The kind of empowerment which has been given to women has several political, social and economic implications. It has created a silent revolution in the country. The reservation itself can only be regarded as the first step in this direction. It is necessary to create proper social, economic and also political conditions to enable women to participate effectively in the local government institutions without endangering the position of the prevailing family system.

The objective of the present enquiry emanates from our argument that empowerment in itself does not work for the emancipation of women. Power without the prerequisite condition for wielding it does not give the expected results. We, therefore, take the provisions of the Act with us and go to empirical field for verification. We shall have opportunity to bring out the gaps in the amendment view and field view.

Let us look at some of the provisions of the amendment. Historically when the Ashok Mehta Committee made a fundamental change in Panchayati Raj for transforming it from an implementing agency to a political institution,[1] it took a long time. In order to implement this recommendation of Ashok Mehta Committee, there was need for constitutional amendment. It, however, took more than a decade for the first steps in this direction to be taken in the form of the Sixty-Fourth Constitutional Amendment Bill which was defeated in Rajya Sabha. In 1992, another legislation, the Seventy-Third Amendment Bill was introduced in Parliament which was adopted in the same year.

There are a few important features of this act:

1. Panchayats will be considered political institution in a truly decentralised structure.
2. The Gram Sabha shall be recognised as the life line of the Panchayats. The voters of the village will constitute its membership. The Panchayat shall be accountable to the Gram Sabha.
3. There will be direct election in all the three tiers of the governance: Gram Panchayat at the village level, taluka or block Panchayat at the intermediate level and Zila Parishad at district level.
4. Insofar as the empowerment of women is concerned, the Act has provided that at least one-third of the total seats at all levels shall be reserved for women of whom one-third shall be from the scheduled castes and scheduled tribes. In this context it is important to note that at least one-third of the total posts of the office bearers at all levels will also be reserved for the women. At empirical plan in tribal areas one-third of the reserved posts would invariably belong to tribal women.
5. Each Panchayat will have a tenure of five years and in case it is dissolved by the state government fresh elections will be held within a period of six months.
6. The elections to local bodies has to be conducted regularly.
7. There will be a separate Election Commission and also a Finance Commission in every State.

8. It is obligatory on the part of the centre as well as the state to provide adequate funds for the Panchayats to enable them to function properly. In addition, the Panchayats will have their own fund raising capacity on the basis of the local resources.
9. Some states like Rajasthan, Haryana, and Orissa have debarred the candidates having more than two children, from contesting in the election with a view to controlling population growth.
10. Some states like those of Bihar, Himachal, Uttar Pradesh, Haryana have the provision of *Nyaya* Panchayat to settle the disputes of all the three levels.

Empowerment in the Amendment

The amendment is considered to be historical in the sense that so far the Constitution has been giving reservation to scheduled castes, scheduled tribes and other Backward classes. Women, however, were given some privilege but it was in the field of reduction of fee and reservation in professional colleges. It is for the first time that women are given reservation of seats at all the levels of Panchayati Raj.

Indian culture and social ethos have all the time been discriminatory against women through the patriarchal system. Though there is prevalence of matriarchy also in some parts of the country, the overall image of women remains that of a discriminated lot of people. It is in this context that the Constitutional Amendment is looked and analysed. The Amendment is not uniformally appreciated all over the country. There is much diversity in the patterns of discrimination of women against men bringing out the differential discrimination. Viduty Mohanty[2] observes:

> 'There are, of course, regional variations (in discrimination) in the northern states the prevailing attitudes is more discriminatory than in southern states. But here again there are notable exceptions as can be seen from widespread female infanticide in certain parts of Tamil Nadu, particularly Salem district. Even dowry taking has registered an increase in certain parts of another southern state, Kerala, which is considered to be a model state insofar as the status of women

in terms of literacy and access to health care facilities is concerned. As a result of these deeply and interesting social attitudes and practices, women by and large have not been independent decision-makers in the country.'

Mohanty has raised the crucial issue when he talks about the power of decision-making. He is right. The Amendment involves women in general and tribal women in particular in the decision-making process. So far so good. Our guess is that even in Panchayati Raj the males would take decisions in a proxy way. But this has to be verified in the field. We do not want any bias in our analysis. We only wished to say that if women really take decisions according to their marital skill, it will go a long way not only in solving the problems of village development but also of our population growth and educational enrolment.

The empowerment which is given in the amendment means that the women will have one-third of the total seats in all the three Panchayati Raj tiers. In other words the women would exercise their decision-making powers in matters of development. Most of the matter fall in the realm of financial management, development administration and educational management. Panchayati Raj has a very comprehensive agenda and in the involvement of the women would give them experience of deciding the matter. In a limited sense women's reservation, would also have socio-cultural dimensions. And this will add to the empowerment content to the women.

Amendment at the State Level

Looking to the federal structure of the Union, the Amendment allows the state to tailor it according to their needs and social forces. We have argued earlier that there is much heterogeneity in gender relations in a country characterised by multi-ethnicities, religions, dialects and customary laws. The state of Rajasthan therefore, has made certain modifications which suit to its genius. We discussed a few such changes brought about by the State of Rajasthan in the Amendment. The state of Rajasthan had a Panchayati Raj which was characterised by the power of implementing the development programmes. This was due to result of Balwant Rai Mehta and Ashok Mehta Committee. With the coming of the Seventy-Third Amendment the state of Rajasthan affected a new tailoring to the Panchayati Raj Institution. This new outfit is known as Rajasthan Panchayati Raj Act, 1994. According to it Gram Sabha at the village level has been given the status of State Assembly. The Gram Sabha is given a statutory status. The Sabha was obliged to state its meetings twice in a year. The membership of Gram Sabha was widespread. It included all the voters finding their place in the voting list. The Secretary of the Panchayat was the Secretary of Gram Sabha. The functions of the Gram Sabha included implementation of development programmes. It was also expected to generate funds through participatory labour or contribution of material in village development. The objective of Gram Sabha was to take steps for Community welfare. Panch and Sarpanch in the Gram Sabha were directly elected. Elections to Pradhan and Up-Pradhan were made by Gram Panchayat members. According to 1994 Act one-third of seats were reserved for women. The women wards were also reserved. The condition of reading and writing for membership to Sarpanch was waved in 1994 Act. This condition was waved perhaps with the acceptation that women would come in a larger wave in Panchayati Raj. According to this Act the Gram Panchayat was entitled to levy taxes. The accountability of the Panchayat also included an audit report of local funds.

1996: Extension of the Earlier Act

The Rajasthan Panchayati Raj Act, 1994 was enacted on 23 April 1994. It was in pursuance of Seventy-Third Constitutional Amendment Act, 1992. As a matter of fact despite the extended Act of 1996, the Act of 1994 is equally applicable to all rural areas of Rajasthan including tribal areas. Change in the Panchayati Act, 1994 was specially brought forth because of the speciality of the tribal society. The extension, therefore, was specific to the tribal society. The Act of 1996 extended the provisions of part Ninth of the Constitution related to Panchayats of the tribal areas. N.K. Singhi has made an elaborate interpretation on the Panchayati Raj (Extension) Act, 1996. The scope of the Extension Act includes the tribal customary laws, social and religious practices and traditional management practices of community resources. The importance of this extension lies in the fact that it takes into consideration the total social profile of the tribals living in the TSP area. We would, for instance, refer to the recognition given by the princely states to traditional laws. In the former Dungarpur state if there was elopement of Bhil girl, the consequent marriage was valid. In the former state of Sirohi if a Grasia married with a girl without paying the bride price, such a marriage was considered valid only when this amount was paid, even if the husband had offspring procreated out of traditional marriage. The extended Act gives due consideration to the customary laws.

Yet another modification in the Panchayati Raj Act (1996) is the crucial problem of defining a village in the tribal context. Tribals live in hamlets, *Phalas* and *Dhani*. How all these settlements could be considered in the Act, was a problem. N.K. Singhi comments on this:

> the criteria for defining a village in the context of tribals would be the character of its being a community implying shared feeling of oneness, sense of territoriality, linkage with part and certain degree of permanency.

The case of a nomadic tribe shall have to be dealt with differently. However their right to being a part of Panchayat cannot be denied.

The third new dimension of the Extension of Act (1996) relates to formalisation of a village into a Gram Sabha. It is necessary to be listed in the electoral role for becoming a member of the Gram Sabha. It means that the voters' list should be made public, for it is the right of every adult member to be a part of the community. The Act in its extension version thus makes a village as a Gram Sabha.

The extension version of Panchayati Raj Act, 1996 is very promising. It has been made at least in the Tribal Sub-Plan Area oriented to the tribal development. It takes into consideration the tribal situation as is found today. The Dilip Singh Bhuria Committee appointed by the Parliament has made a logical case for giving due consideration to the tribal customary laws. The customary laws are the treasure of the earlier experiences of tribal people. If, they are made adoptive to the Panchayat Act, the Bhuria Committee believed, the tribals will have greater incorporation in the mainstream of development. The new form of Act has taken these laws in consideration.

Panchayati Raj Act Get Further Modified

The State of Rajasthan has further made some changes in the Extension Act, 1996. Despite a few changes, there are two major modifications which have relevance for our study that is empowerment of women. The Act has still now, i.e., at the time of our writing (February, 2000) not got the consent of Assembly and remains an ordinance only. But it shows the will of the Governor of the state. If a woman at all the three tiers of the Panchayati Raj resigns voluntarily or is ousted because of no-confidence or some irregularity, *she would be replaced by a women candidate only.* A male candidate in such a situation is no alternative. Such a provision in the Act further strengthens the power of woman that she has no alternative. She is a must. Any conspiracy or politics cannot replace a woman member.

Another change in the ordinance is that a member is disqualified if, he or she has more than two offsprings. This disability would work as a deterrence on population growth. Such a measure is beneficial for a woman as she will not have to mother more than two children. This disqualification was there in the earlier Panchayati Raj Act. But it involved an elaborate procedure to enable the court to disqualify the man. The power of disqualification is now given to the Panchayati Raj tiers and the moment it is reported that a third life has seen the light of the day, the member is disqualified.

The ordinance on the extended version of Panchayati Raj (1994) provides a wider exposure to women. Gram Sabha ordinarily is a huge group of members. It provides lesser opportunities for women to articulate themselves. But the new form gives ward the status of Gram Sabha. Ward is a familiar phenomenon for women. They can express themselves at this level easily. And, therefore, the ordinance of Panchayati Raj, at least, theoretically provides a greater space to tribal women for decision-making.

One very powerful input which the ordinance has put is that in all cases, notwithstanding any election, the heads of Gram Panchayat, Panchayat Samiti and Zila Parishad of TSP area would invariably be the tribals. The status of Tribal thus becomes dominant for their being at the helm of affair. Such a provision was non-existent in the earlier version of Panchayati Raj Act.

Methodological Approach

The logic of present enquiry is empirical-historical. We have not adopted a statistical model to present our data. The approach has been to develop cognition about Panchayati Raj through our own experience and this is how we turn empiricism. Empiricism in a broader way is experience. We codified our experience in qualitative categories. And because of this that the study generates cognitive statements about the consequences of women empowerment. Though the Act or the Ordinance only shows that there is a positive incorporation of tribal women in the structure and functioning of Panchayati Raj, obviously it all means a revolution in the gender relations. Gender issues are now live problems of urban, literate and industrial societies. It has become a relevant problem for tribal gender relations also. Because it provides a new role model to the backward women. In the context of urban-industrial society, the gender problems of rural tribal women are altogether different. It is in this context that we design our inquiry within historical perspective also.

For intensive study we have taken certain steps to provide an edge to gender problems. Before putting our pen to work we made a thorough study to know what is happening in the area of empowerment of women. It cannot be gainsaid that there is any dearth of women study. During the last two decades so many women studies have been conducted that there is virtual flood of these studies in social sciences. Every woman worth her salt styles herself as an emancipator of gender discrimination. However, there is much lack of theoretical input of such women's studies. We will take note of some major studies which discussed the consequences of women empowerment.

At the outset we would strike a note. Empowerment issue is a popular issue for social sciences. Male chauvinism is the focal point of discussion in most of the women studies. But the work output of empowerment input has hardly been linked in such studies. We admit there is no single reason to cause an effect in social behaviour. There are reasons for social behaviour. And among reasons there are some effective reasons for a particular cause which need to be identified. In this connection we would refer to one very interesting study conducted in the field of Sustainable Development Debate which takes into consideration the whole problem with feminist perspective. The book is an edited version of articles taken from different sources.[3] The work argues that much of the writings in the domain of development do not take into consideration the deteriorating status of women. For instance, when environment is decayed, most of the burden falls on the women. It is they who are obliged to collect fuel from far off places and street to street. All the contributors to the volume look at the development programme from a feminist perspective.

There is yet another study which is purely a theoretical contribution to feminism.[4] The contributors to this volume examine feminism as a theoretical issue. Whenever the status of women in contemporary society is discussed naturally the theme goes to power analysis. According to these authors theory is a form of strategy. And strategy involves recognizing the situation and alignment of power for and against which it operates. It must be said that the contributor of this volume are not perspective wise functioners. The Marxist point of view is also been equally discussed. Interestingly the views of post-modernists such as Jacque Lacan have also been incorporated in the study.

In such a context Foucault and Althusser also find a dominant place. The legal position of women particularly those related to rural life has also been subjected to analysis. This work severely criticised the gender role in Constitution. It is here that we find the observation of leftist writer A.R. Desai.[5]

Closely related to the above mentioned study edited by Shirin and Geraldine, there is yet another work well grounded in theory.[6] In this work the author has made a conceptual exercise and discusses at length feminism, emancipation, liberation, sex-gender system and finally patriarchy. The very glaring weakness of the work is that in defining the concepts the author has shown her swing only on Western women world. The writer has not taken the status situation of women. What is worse, her theoretical analysis totally neglects the tribal women.

Yet a new arrival which raises certain interesting issues is that of feminism and politics. The book is worked out by Indian editors, Chandra Talpade, Mohinty and Rueso Lourdes.[7] The book stands on post-modern perspective and analyses the gender status of Third World women. The terminology used by the contributors is drawn from the bit of post-modernism. The problem of gender relations is taken to be very serious in Western world compared to Third World countries. The focus of gender rests on family, work place and religious network.

Neira Desai and her colleague Maihtrey Krishanraj have edited a book on women and society in India. The two authors are basically sociologist and have tried to establish relationship between women and society. In taking up this exercise the authors have tried to find out how social changes in society have affected women's position, specially the development process. The forces of economy, growth of education, structure of family have been taken for analysis. Analysing the negative impact of democracy the book reads:[8]

> There are various action strategies for change whose impact has been both positive and negative. Democratic rights granted in principle are nullified by women's subordinate status. The process of development has increasingly separated the public from private and has enlarged the public sphere with more informal institutions against the earlier more informal community, caste, neighbourhood, institutions. Public institution often provide scope for women to escape from traditional constraints.

Some empirical kind of work has also been done by Indian women social scientists. For instance Beena Agarwal[9] has made some very insightful studies in Indian agriculture. She is concerned with the work participation of rural women in the Third World. She also examines empirically women, poverty and agricultural growth. One of her very interesting study is about tribal matriliny in transition. The empirical investigations in this case are carried out in North-East India. It is here that she takes up the gender issues. Her major theme of analysis is the land rights of women in South Asia. In one of her case study she refers to the statement of landless women which runs as below:

> We want arable land, all the rest is humbug.... Please go and ask the *Sarkar* (Government) why, when it distributes land,

> we don't get a title. Are we not peasants? If my husband throws me out, what is my security?

Subaltern historians have done some significant work in the area of gender relationship. The historians look at the gender problem with a perspective of grass-roots level. Shaheed Amin and Dipesh Chakrawarty have taken a stock of the situation of low level people in the caste hierarchy. They refer to the B.L. Mandal's report and the Prime Ministership of V.P. Singh during the year 1990. In their conclusion they observe: [10]

> It seems to us that the early 1990s represent a turning point for Indian feminism. Each of the metonyms we have chosen for analysis focus on hegemonic mobilisations of a feminist subject specific to our times. Each displayed the contradictions that emerge within feminist politics and the challenges they confront gender analysis in the context of the refiguring of dominance in a rapidly globalising Indian economy.

The finding of Shaheed and Dipesh are quite interesting in the sense that they make certain generalisation which have a bearing on the emerging domination of women. However the subaltern historians as the tradition they have developed do not stress on empiricism. The historians hardly do field work and this amply applies on subaltern historians.

Political scientists have also sought to delineate the status of women in politics. The thesis of this category of political scientists is to identify the role of women in political decision-making fields of nation's life. One such study is that of Susheela Patni who has carried out an empirical study on the role of women in Vidhan Sabha. She has generated data through caste studies and interview. She also looks at the role of women in Local Self-Government. She observes:[11]

> Women are conscious of the manifold nuances of articulated involvement in political life. *Whereas numerically their access to decision-making apparatus is hardly encouraging, there is no dearth of their concern for gender justice and cognition of responsibility and obligations in this regard.*

Susheela's study, truly speaking, gives ample data regarding legislative matters relating to Vidhan Sabha. But she never provides any insight on matters related to discrimination of women against men. And how gender relations emerge and create complications in Vidhan Sabha.

We would not further elaborate any analytical studies referring to the status of women. It is interesting to discuss here a matter of theoretical content in terms of *women's status* and *gender relations*. In both the terms there is a difference of emphasis. Social scientists have long been trying to discuss the status of women. By status *they mean the position of women in the society at large.* Here the emphasis is on the status relating to society. But when the social scientists discuss gender relations, they stress on the relations between males and females in terms of discrimination. Thus it is the discrimination which distinguishes gender study from status study. We would now, therefore, refer to a few studies which have a bearing on gender and Panchayati Raj.

Poornima Vyasulu and Vinod Vyasulu have identified the gender role at Panchayati Raj.[12] The Vyasulus in this study emphasised the participation of women in social development. They discussed the structure of Panchayati Raj System in Karnataka and the experiences of women in it. At the close of the study, the authors identify the barriers or impediments which the women encounter in the political process. The findings of the study do not bring any good news to feminists. The Vyasulus conclude:

> Much more will be needed if gender justice is to become the norm. And it will take time. We must not be impatient. But it is important to support this fledgling experiment in every way we can if we believe in democracy at the grass-roots.

Yet another study which refers to gender issues is that from South and South-East Asia is by Leela Dube.[13] Leela Dube is an anthropologist by profession. She specialises in matrilineal society and that leads her to write about Kerala women. She does not discuss gender relations with reference to wielding of power. Her focus is on gender relations in the context of kinship patterns. She is very systematic in depicting the implications of gender differences. As indicated, Leela Dube does not touch on power relations. But on theoretical plane concludes that stability in marriage is more valuable in the rights and lives of women. In other words if women grouse always for their rights and privileges in the realm of family and marriage, there would come instability in the family life.

We have taken a stock of few studies pertaining to empowerment of women and the related gender relations only to identify some areas which we could plug to formulate our present enquiry and fill the gaps in the field of empowerment.

We hold in categorical terms that we are not victims to the craze of which has come in social sciences to write about empowerment. Neither are we interested to find implications of empowerment in gender relationship. Our basic object is to plug the gaps in the contemporary studies and construct our enquiry in a systematic way. The studies, surely a few only that we have taken for review indicate that most of the findings are oriented to the status of women *vis-a-vis* the surrounding society. But how has empowerment at Panchayat level that is grass-root level effected change in gender relations, has not been touched by the current social science study. We would struggle to seek an answer to this question at the empirical plane.

The present enquiry has its field of universe consists of the four districts of TSP area. Earlier we included Sirohi district also as a part of our study. Later on when we made first trip to our field, we found that Bhils do not constitute any habitation in Sirohi district. It is the home land of Gracia tribe. We have, therefore, operationally restricted our research to four districts only—Udaipur, Dungarpur, Banswara and Chittorgarh. For intensive study we have drawn purposively four Panchayat Samities, one each from the four districts of TSP area. Thus for Udaipur district we have taken Kotra Panchayat Samiti. It is in the remotest part of the district and inhabits women who had long remained encapsulated in hills and forests. The Bhils here are not only late comers to education, they have come to know about education only a recently.

In the district of Dungarpur our sample consists of Simalwara Panchayat Samiti. It is close to Dungarpur-Ahmedabad Road and has a good number of caste Hindus living close to tribals. The Samiti though numerically dominated by tribals has enough influence of Brahmins and Jains. Simalwara thus presupposes a better stock of tribal women. Similar is the characteristic profile of the Bhils and Bhil women of Panchayat Samiti Ghatol which is within Banswara district. Political awakening in Ghatol is heartening. It has developed on the lines of modern township. It is the seat of weekly market; it has a cinema house and its market is quite flourishing.

Chittorgarh district has only two Panchayat Samities that of Pratapgarh and Arnodh which are in TSP area. There was a time when Pratapgarh had the status of a district soon after the merger of princely state. Arnodh on the other hand, is a religious centre having the pilgrim centre of Gautamji, well-known in south Rajasthan. Every year it draws a large number of people who visit the sacred caves of the Rishi Gautam. This has provided an exposure to the people of Arnodh diverse groups of caste Hindus.

Thus our universe of study for intensive enquiry has four Panchayat Samities. At the outset we have mentioned that we have tried to make this study an empirical monograph. This way we take a departure from quantification of data. We have generated qualitative data and have tried to make some generalisation out of this empiricism. To generate data we have made insight studies at all the three tiers of Panchayati Raj. At the lowest level we have restricted ourselves to the Sarpanch, and the Ward Panch. Notwithstanding the kind of membership at Panchayat level we have discussed our problem with as many members as were available to us. But interview with Sarpanch was indispensable to us. Thus we have studied only women Sarpanchas distributed over the Panchayat Samiti of our sample. At the Panchayat Samiti level also, the women Pradhan and the members of Panchayat Samiti have also been in the similar way interviewed by us. At the apex level that is Zila Parishad the notable members and women Zila Parishad members have been contacted and interviewed in a focused way. We have not restricted ourselves to female members only. The males also have their cognition about women members. Our interviews with the Panchayati Raj members have, therefore, been balanced. Not only non-officials, the officials and the villagers at large have been randomly chosen by us for information. The sample group thus for us has been a mixed group, one can call it a heterogeneous group. The data which we discussed here are those which have resulted out of our field work. It would be interesting to say that we have passed all our holidays in the tribal field mentioned above.

Notes and References

1. Mathews, George, *Status of Panchayati Raj in India*, Concept Publishing House, New Delhi, 1995.
2. Mohanty, Viduty, 'Panchayati Raj, Seventy-Third Constitutional Amendment and Women', *Economic and Political Weekly*, December 13, 1995, p. 3346.
3. Warcourt, Wendy (ed.), *Feminist Perspective on Sustainable Development*, Zed Books, London and New Jersey, 1994.
4. Gurew Suneja, *Feminist Knowledge: Critique and Construct*, Routledge, London, 1990.
5. Shirin M. Rai and Livesley Geraldine (eds.), *Women and the State: International Perspective*, London, 1996.
6. Lerner Gerda, *The Creation of Patriarchy*, Oxford University Press, 1993.
7. Mohanty, Chandra, Talpade and Lurdes Rueso, *Third World Women and the Feminism*, Indiana University Press, Bloomington, 1991.
8. Desai, Neera and Krishnaraj Maihtry, *Women and Society in India*, Ajanta, New Delhi, 1987.
9. Agarwal, Beena, 'Work Participation of Rural Women in Third World: Some Data and Conceptual Biases', *Economic and Political Weekly*, December 21-29, 1985.

   Tribal Matriliny in Transition: Gender, Property, Production Relations in North-East India', Paper for ILO, Geneva, 1990.

   A Field of One's Own: Gender and Land Rights in South Asia, Cambridge University Press, Cambridge, 1994.
10. Amin, Shaheed and Chakrawarty, Dipesh, *Subaltern Studies*, IX, Oxford University Press, Oxford, 1996, p. 260.
11. Patni, Shusheela, *Women Political Elite*, (Search for Identity), Printwell, Jaipur, 1994, p. 118.
12. Vyasulu, Poornima, Vyasulu, Vinod, 'Women in Panchayati Raj: Grass-Roots Democracy in Malgudi', *Economic and Political Weekly*, December 25, 1999.
13. Dube, Leela, *Women and Kinship, Comparative Perspectives on Gender in South and South-East Asia*, Vistaar Publications, New Delhi, 1997.

CHAPTER 5

Grass-roots of Panchayati Raj: The Tribal Women

The empowerment of women in the Panchayati Raj has the basic objective to involve women in development action. If we analyse the development programmes assigned for Panchayati Raj, in TSP Area, we would find that the programmes are of three categories. First, there are programmes which are for the development of the tribal area. These programmes are actually programmes initiated and supported by the Central Government. In such programmes the financial burden is divided on the basis of fifty-fifty. In some cases the Central Government has the total responsibility of spending the money.

The second category of programmes are individual beneficiaries programmes. The beneficiary programmes could be categorised under three heads: one, education, two irrigation and three training, within the framework of these beneficiary programmes. The tribals are entitled to take benefits which they find suitable for themselves. However, it must be said that those who are in a position to take the benefit, can only avail themselves of it. For instance those who have their own irrigation facilities, can avail benefit only by the individual beneficiary programme. But on the other hand, one does not have any well or say a land for cultivation cannot benefit through this category of programmes. In the long run one can argue that those who are marginal farmers cannot benefit from these programmes. In a tribal situation it is possible that some of the individual beneficiary programmes only get exploited by those who are in the category of middle class peasant.

The third category of development programmes are those which are floated, as a result of the celebration of fifty years of India's independence. These programmes are meant to help the tribals to generate employment for themselves. Actually the programmes are self-employed programmes. The earlier TRYSEM programmes and other welfare programmes are included in the self-employment programmes. As a matter of fact the earlier programmes are cancelled. And the new programmes popularly known as SGSY are put into operation.

The above three categories of programmes is at present in operation in the tribal area. It is important at this stage to mention that the Panchayati Raj involves the women members including the males to take decision about the successful implementation of the programmes. The programme implementation and the related decision-making basically rests with the Gram Sabha. It is emphasised that Gram Sabha is the counterpart of Legislative Assembly at the Gram Sabha level. The Panchayati Raj legislation has worked out the functions of the three tiers of Panchayati Raj in terms of distribution of work. Before we discuss the role of women members *vis-a-vis* the male members, let us find out the development work distribution according to the three tiers.

Gram Sabha and Its Role in Development Activities

According to Art 3 of Rajasthan Panchayati Raj Act implemented from April 9, 1994 the Gram Sabha is empowered to take up a large number of activities. Its overall function is to help in the implementation of all the activities of the Panchayati Raj notwithstanding its category. For instance whether the activity is of educational development or irrigation facilities, it is obligatory on the part of Gram Panchayat to bring the scheme to its implementation. One very important function of Gram Sabha is to identify the numbers who had to be included for benefits of particular programmes. If subsidy is to be given to a peasant below the poverty line, the Gram Sabha would help the administrators to identify people or peasant coming within this category.

One very important development activity in the Sabha is to provide infrastructure facility. The school building needs to be extended to accommodate the rising admission role of students. The extension of building is made in cash or kind contribution of the members of Gram Sabha. In such a contributory situation it becomes obligatory for Gram Sabha members to motivate people to contribute their share.

Yet another important activity of Panchayati Raj is to promote the cause of adult education. Without the co-operation of the village people the adult classes can hardly be run successfully. In this field of development Gram Sabha has to contribute enough. And particularly if women members come forward, women adult education programme can be turned into a successful story. What is important in the successful running of adult classes is that the Gram Sabha should translate the adult education as their own programme and not imposed from outside. Second, the teachers-in-charge of adult classes are notorious for playing truant in running the classes. Normally they are irregular in attending the classes or they are absent without availing of any leave. The adult classes have been run in this old fashion of neglect and avoidance. Now under the new Act any member of the Gram Sabha can raise his finger against the erring teachers. This is a very important responsibility which has come to the members of Gram Sabha.

Village India traditionally is known for its unity. In all occasions of sorrow and pleasures the villagers have exhibited their unity. This unity now is characterised by factionalism and in some cases religious sectarianism. The harmony and unity of the village has now been made the responsibility of Gram Sabha. In other words the Gram Sabha has to work across the caste, class and religious boundaries. The earlier approach to development was monolith. Development was considered to be an activity of the Panchayat Samiti. It was the government programme considered to be imposed by development administrator. This kind of mindset has been set at rest by the present Act. Whenever there is any threat to the harmony and peace of the village, it becomes obligatory for the Gram Sabha to summon its meeting and make all efforts to come out of the crisis.

On a broader plan all the development activities have to be approved and sanctioned by the Gram Sabha. The Gram Panchayat cannot initiate any development programme without taking the consent and seeking the confidence of Gram Sabha. If at any stage of the implementation of development programmes some shortcomings emerge the matter has to be referred to the Gram Panchayat. It will be the responsibility of Vikas Adhikari or his nominee to work as an associate to the meeting of Gram Sabha. One very important privilege of Gram Sabha is to constitute a Vigilance Committee which would take into consideration the decisions of Gram Sabha and find out that these are properly implemented. The Vigilance Committee would consists of those members who enjoy the confidence of the masses at large.

1. *Some Voluntary Development Work to be Taken Over by Gram Sabha of TSP Area*

The rights and privileges of Gram Sabha are very wide. As a matter of fact Gram Sabha within the provisions of the Act can develop according to its own genus. It is autonomous so far its reform activities are concerned. We would discuss here a few of the activities which the Gram Sabha can initiate and promote within its territory:

1. *Prohibition on Liquor.* If the Gram Sabha realizes that there has been much of liquor drinking in the village and the females including the families find themselves threatened, they can decide to prohibit liquor drinking. This is all a local problem and the Gram Sabha being a grass-root organisation can bring it within control. Prohibition of liquor does not go against the Directive Principles of the State Policy. In other words if a measure does not violate the tenets of Constitution, the Gram Sabha can be advised to implement such a policy.

2. *Minor Forest Produce.* Forest has been friend and philosopher for the tribals. Their relations have through the ages been friendly and therefore one very phenomenal privilege which the Act has given to tribals is to regulate the collection of minor forest produce (MFP) from the neighbouring forest. The regulation of MFP is in the hands of Gram Sabha. There would not be any intervention from the state government. In other words, minor forest produce become the asset of the Gram Sabha only.

3. *Land Encroachment.* Truly, in the past tribal land was the property of the community itself. Now the land has become the property of the state. But the state cannot put the land in its pockets and relax. After all in practice the land belongs to the people themselves. Such an idiom has been translated by the Panchayati Raj Act and the Gram Sabha is given rights to check any land encroachment in the village. There is a common practice in the village to grab the community land by political influence or money

power. The Gram Sabha is entitled to take action through the Vigilance Committee or its members to check encroachment.

2. *Customary System*

The development programmes which are implemented in the society are new for them. But the Act takes records to traditional customary practices and argue that the programmes may be implemented within the traditional framework of customary laws. For instance if a stud bull is given to a village for improving the cattle breed the villagers should be given an understanding through the content of the traditional stud bull kept by each village. Locally such bulls are called *Surat no Sand*. Such a bull goes untouched by the whole village. If the improved breed of stud bull is introduced in the village through the context of such a tradition, it is likely to be accepted by the people. What is required of Gram Sabha is to establish a nexus between the village traditions and the new programmes.

The Act envisages that if a family is advanced loan by the Samiti under a scheme and the family does not pay back, the Gram Sabha should take it as its responsibility to persuade family to pay back the loan. It has to be emphasised that Government loans are for the welfare of people and need to be accepted in the same spirit. We have a field work experience among the Bhils of Banswara district. A *Bania* of a village in his capacity as a trader advanced a loan of Rupees two hundred to a Bhil farmer. He did not pay back the loan. For the fault of a single family, the trader stopped advancing loan to all the members of the village. It was an unexpected step. The people assembled and shared the amount of loan individually and the amount so collected was handed over to the trader and it had a spectacular impact on the trader. The credit for the whole village was revised and the defaulter family had to hang his head low. Thus the customary laws have a great strength. And they should be applied in the development of the programmes.

3. *Programmes of Education and Health*

The programmes of education and health services are very wide and multiple in the TSP area. The government administration can hardly control and supervise all these programmes. True, these services are paid by the government but the Gram Sabha should take it on itself to implement these programmes according to their stipulated scope. The Gram Sabha has delegated powers to supervise the implementation of the programme. The school programmes are introduced by the Panchayat. But if the teacher does not attend the school, he neglects his classes and plays truant, it is the responsibility of Gram Sabha to see that necessary discipline is observed by the Panchayat employees. Again in the case of Public Health Centre (PHC) if the doctor does not open the centre and provide his services, Gram Sabha has to keep a vigil on the working of the centre. Punishing the defaulters should be within the powers of the Gram Sabha. It should see that education and health services are properly made available to the people at large.

4. *Water Resources*

Irrigation facilities are with the state government. The government, if resources permit, may construct small and big dams. But the Gram Sabha can identify the small water resources which are locally available. There are some states who have very successfully managed watershed arrangements. The Panchayati Raj Act has given powers to Gram Sabha in scheduled area of Rajasthan to make watershade arrangements. This is a happy augury and the indigenous knowledge of the people being very rich, can enable them this aspect of irrigation facilities. Not only this the Gram Sabha can also take steps to provide potable water for drinking for villagers.

5. *Minor Minerals*

There are a few tribals who can be entrusted with the work of minor minerals. As a matter of fact the mining department looks after issuing the leases to minor minerals for instance in the hilly region of Rajasthan. There is availability of building stone. Similarly there could also be some minerals which are used in the cement factories. The Panchayati Raj Act in this respect has two benefits which can be given to the local people. It is the state government which grant leases. But the Gram Sabha can recommend the prospecting of minerals before the formal licence is issued by the state department. Second, the Gram Sabha in the scheduled area is also given plenary powers for the recommendation of concession in leases to the state mining department.

The above two powers namely water resources and minor minerals go in line with the tribal traditions. It is argued that the tribals have been residing in hills and forests. This provides natural resources to the people. The government should not be allowed as far as possible to make profit of these resources. The tribals have a strong sense of building a friendly environment. And they have a natural right and a priority to fulfil their needs. The Act has taken this in consideration.

6. *Delegation of Supervising Development Programmes in the TSP Area*

The Gram Sabha is also given power to keep a vigil on all the local development scheme. The district headquarters and so are the Samiti headquarters a lesser distant away from the Gram Sabha. It is the Gram Sabha which is on the spot and therefore it should wield its powers to see the proper implementation of all such development activities.

The role of Gram Sabha in the Panchayati Raj development activities is very large. It is given power to supervise and control all the development activities. There are a few important functions which have been given to the Gram Sabha. As a matter of fact Gram Sabha is made competent to safeguard and preserve the traditions and customs of the people, their cultural identity, communitarian sources and the customary mode of dispute resolution to put it in short. We may say that some of the special provisions made for Gram Sabha included enforcement of prohibition, protection of community land, acquisition of land, collection of minor forest produce, management of water resources, regulation of village markets and control over loan cases to tribals. What is important is that the approval of development programmes before implementation is required from the Gram Sabha. It is the Gram Sabha which puts its seal on the identification and selection of beneficiaries. If there are oustees from a minor dam construction, Gram Sabha is taken into confidence for rehabilitating them. Finally it is the Gram Sabha which has the full control over the social sectors of the tribal communities.

Gram Panchayat and Its Development Privileges

After the Seventy-Third Amendment both the structure and functioning of Gram Panchayat have been strengthened. Practically Gram Panchayat is identified and recognised as a distinctive institution. Structurally the members elected for Gram Sabha constitute the Gram Panchayats. B.D. Sharma though a bureaucrat has recently been deep-rooted in village realities argues that the Gram Panchayat is responsible for the working of all the Gram Sabhas falling within its jurisdiction. However the Gram Panchayat cannot interfere in the independent working of the Gram Sabhas. On the other hand the proposals made by Gram Panchayats would be screened by the Gram Sabha. Interestingly any person who has some grudge against the decisions of Gram Sabha can appeal to the Gram Panchayats. The internal disputes of Gram Sabha are intervened, negotiated and settled by Gram Panchayats. In performing such a delicate job the Gram Panchayat can seek the assistance of elderly persons. This would be a kind of a village council including the members of Gram Panchayats, Gram Sabha and village experts. The decision of the village council would be called in the traditional paraphase the decision of the Panchas. It would be something like the decision of Panch Parmeshwar as is mentioned in the classic story of Munshi Prem Chand—*Panch Parmeshwar*.

Membership to Gram Panchayat is through direct elections. It is constituted by ward Panch and Sarpanch. The head of Gram Panchayat is designated as Sarpanchas. Theoretically the Sarpanch and also the other members of Gram Panchayat are accountable to the Gram Sabha or to the village society at large. The Act has elaborated the powers of Gram Panchayats. If, there is an honest enumeration of all the subjects assigned under the Gram Panchayat it would amount for 33 items. On a broader plane it could be said that the rights of the Gram Panchayat are very comprehensive and elaborate. They are more than exhaustive. However, these powers for the purpose of analysis can be categorised into three:

1. Civic amenities,
2. Social welfare activities, and
3. Development work.

Civic Amenities

Normally what Municipalities do in the realm of civic amenities is expected to be done by Gram Panchayat. It appears that the framers of the Act are much obsessed by urban community life. They have included street lighting village road and amenities of this kind in this category. Factuality of the village life does not find a place of status in this category. For instance, the villages which have some experience of development in the field of tap water supply find that there is no proper drainage system as an outlet for water. Problems of this kind resulting from development programmes do not constitute a part of the power of Gram Panchayats. However the provision of amenities give a direction to the Samiti to take care of it.

The Act entitles the Gram Panchayat for maintaining the sanitation, street lighting, maintenance of village roads and schools, supply of drinking water to the Gram Panchayats. These constitute the civil functions.

Social Welfare Activities

These activities include maintenance of burning and burial grounds, keeping the statistics of birth and death, establishment of child welfare and maternity centre, control of cattle ponds, propagation of family planning and promotion of agriculture. It is the prime duty of the Gram Panchayat to encourage agriculture. Horticulture also constitutes an additional area of generating new income in the village. The Gram Panchayat is expected to identify the barren land of the locality and convert it to agricultural land. Proper maintenance of pasture land also falls within the powers of the Gram Panchayat.

Development of Work

When the Panchayats do some development works then they act as the agent of the Panchayat Samiti. The development activities are very exhausting. These activities on one hand provide infrastructure to the community and on the other hand extend the net of individual beneficiary programmes. The overall objective of development activities is to remove the poverty of the tribal people. This can be done by enabling the villagers to generate new income in the family.

The development activities of the Panchayat include the construction of roads, public building, the wells, tanks, schools, Panchayat houses, library rooms, promotion of co-operative societies, looking after minor irrigation works and several other activities which promote the people to take to an appreciable way of life.

Though the Act has enumerated most of activities which can be taken over by Panchayat, much is left to the vision of the members. As a matter of fact the framers of Panchayati Raj have provided a development blueprint which can be translated into action by the Gram Panchayat. But the local reality and the felt needs of the people are best realised by the Gram Panchayat. The Act is very wide in its scope and if some development actions can really fulfil the needs of the people the Gram Panchayat has a free hand to take up the issue.

Resource Structure of Gram Panchayat

The list of activities to be performed by the Gram Panchayat is much exhaustive. But nothing substantial can be done without adequate resources. When Gandhiji talked about Gram Swarajya and self-reliance, he had objective in mind that the villages should develop their own resources. If the resources flow from outside the reliance would go out of the window. To give sustainable flow to development some resources have to be created at the village level. The framers of Panchayati Raj have tried to give a limited autonomy to exploit local resources to the people.

A few steps are envisaged to create local resources. For instance, Gram Panchayats are authorised to levy certain taxes at their own level. Levying of taxes for certain resources are enumerated. A Gram Panchayat can tax on property, profession and also can levy taxes on animals and vehicles. Panchayats are also empowered to levy some other taxes and fees like octroi, tax on shop, fees for the use of rest houses, drainage fees, light rate, water rate, and other such items of village life. The Panchayat can also derive income from their property, investment, certain undertakings and public contributions. In addition to these resources the funds received from the state government constitute a major part of the Gram Panchayat income.

Activities of Panchayat Samities

It is the second important tier of the Panchayati Raj. In the earlier Panchayati Raj Act members to the Panchayat Samiti were elected indirectly. The Sarpanchas who come from the Gram Panchayat directly elected from the people, constituted the Samiti membership. They among themselves elected the Pradhan. Thus in the earlier Act the Pradhan of the Samiti did not have any involvement of the people in a direct way. In the present Panchayati Raj Act the members of the Panchayat Samiti are directly elected by the people. These elected members elect their Pradhan and Up-pradhan. In such a situation the Samiti members and Pradhan cannot have their traditional homogenic influence. One third membership to Panchayat Samiti is reserved for women. This makes the entry of women a compulsory phenomenon. They can sit with the males and put their points of view. In a tribal dominated sub-plan area most of the members of Panchayat Samities are tribals. Their monopolistic right is now shared by the reserved seats of the women. This is, to say the least, a fundamental change in the structure of Panchayat Samiti. One more feather to this structure, the Pradhan in the Samiti in all cases is from the one-third lot of women reservation. So far numerical strength is concerned, the Panchayat Samiti has one-third of its members as women.

The structure of Panchayat Samiti in the new form of Panchayati Raj is such that the members who are directly elected to it have their say. In other words the villages are represented to Panchayat Samiti on a direct election basis. Earlier the Sarpanchas were the members of the Samiti and they could get their things done here. Now they do not have any such place. Panchayat Samiti has a direct nexus with the villages. The Panchayat Samiti is a powerful body because it is through it that the development programmes are allocated and executed. The funds received by the district collector are handed over to Zila Pramukh who directs it to Panchayat Samiti. The Vikas Adhikari is the government executive who helps the non-officials—Pradhan, in doing the technical work and helping him or her to follow the administrative line.

It is in the Panchayat Samiti that the women members can exercise their powers. For instance in the TSP area of Rajasthan there are on an average 24 members. Out of which eight are women members. Generally the size of membership in a Panchayat Samiti varies with the member of Gram Panchayat. In our study the membership size varies from 15 to 38. In such a composition it is not difficult for women members to get their proposal through if they work unitedly. This is a theoretical situation we shall have occasion later on to report the actual functioning of the Samiti. At this stage of discussion it is quite clear that the women get empowered and if they want to create erosion in the discrimination which they suffer at the grass-root levels, they can wield their power. Thus the framers of Panchayati Raj Act are justified in empowering women.

Functions of the Panchayat Samiti

The functioning of Panchayat Samiti can be seen at two levels. First, the financial level of the Samiti is very important. Generally the finances received from the State and Central Government come to Panchayat Samiti. But the Samiti develops its own resources for local development works. They can levy certain taxes and also receive some share of the land revenue and grant from the government. It must be observed here that the Samities which constitute our sample groups of TSP areas have a numerical strength of tribals. As a matter of fact the tribal population in the districts of Dungarpur and Banswara varies between sixty and seventy per cent to the general population. In the Panchayat Samities of these two districts, the tribal members have a numerical dominance. Same is the case for the two Samities of Chittorgarh. In the Kotra Panchayat Samiti of Udaipur district there is only one non-tribal members to the total Samiti membership. It goes without saying that at the Samiti level the tribals are free to decide their own course of development within the budgetary provision given to it.

The Panchayat Samiti officer is the chief executive officer and under him are various extension officers, village level workers and other clerical staff. The Panchayat Samiti exercises administrative control over the Vikas Adhikari.

The major objective of Panchayat Samiti is to bring the different development programme to ground. But there is one more routine activity of the Samiti. It is a kind of planning office. All the schemes are planned here. Theoretically it sounds well in the sense that it is the Panchayat Samiti which identifies the needs of the people. It makes a plan for it, its strategy and its outputs but more often than not, schemes come in a ready-made way from centre and state also. The locally sponsored schemes generally get defeated in terms of non-viability and inadequacies of funds with the state government. But the schemes from the state and centre are accepted by Samiti 'as a given programme'.

The Panchayati Raj Act has enumerated a long list of the activities which the Samiti is obliged to implement. In terms of number the Samiti has thirty odd activities in its bit to be performed in a systematic way. For the purpose of providing a focus to village development we would prepare catalogue of these activities as under:

1. Agriculture and Land Reforms

Green revolution came into existence in 1967 and afterwards. Its first arrival was in the state of Punjab followed by Haryana, Maharashtra, Gujarat, Tamil Nadu and other states. In the state of Rajasthan it has been a late comer. This is also largely due to the fact that a larger portion of land is covered by arid zone. The TSP area is hilly topography. Even then the Act has provided some measures which can encourage the arrival of Green Revolution. The TSP area has one major dam Mai Bajaj Sagar Dam and Jakham Dam in Banswara and Udaipur districts respectively. There are a few minor dams also. The land is fertile. There is enough opportunities for the Samities to consolidate Green Revolution.

Within the agricultural activities of the Panchayat Samiti there are programmes to develop horticulture besides increasing the agricultural produce. Horticulture is a new area of development. Some fruits and vegetables can be grown within this programme. The Panchayat Samiti has been given sufficient scope for introducing High Yielding Varieties (HYV) in the respective area. In the field of agriculture improved seeds and manures have to be promoted to usher in the Green Revolution. What is important is that the Panchayat Samiti should take steps to provide credit facilities within its jurisdiction. Generally the co-operative movement has failed in Rajasthan and on the other hand it has come out successful in the neighbouring state of Gujarat. If the Panchayat Samities have any motivation and will to enhance the co-operative network, the Act provides enough possibilities.

The region of south Rajasthan has an agricultural university. The Panchayat Samities can learn enough in the skills of agriculture from the university. The Samiti is empowered to send its peasants for training to the university. It is through the university that the new crops can be taken up by the tribal peasants. Soyabean is one such new crop that has been learned by Banswara peasant from university. The Act has provided all options to the Samiti for paving the way for Green Revolution. The role of women in agriculture can also be improved if technology is replaced for manual sowing and harvesting.

2. Agricultural Management

It is difficult indeed to provide viable sources of irrigation in a hilly terrain. Canal irrigation is suitable for plains. In hilly region the wells, anicuts and watershade arrangements are suitable. No tailor made set of irrigation facility can work at the local level. It is here that the Panchayat Samiti has to take crucial decisions. In a single Samiti it is possible to take different strategies for watershade management. The Samiti if the topography allows can plan for minor dams or anicuts. The framers of Panchayati Raj Act have shown enough wisdom in allowing the Samiti to sort out its own alternative of irrigation. We know that in the Samities of Dungarpur and Udaipur the choice has gone for digging wells. The district of Dungarpur is very well-known in TSP area for the digging of wells. In Banswara, on the other hand, canal water irrigation and anicut irrigation are popular. Watershade management in this respect is very intelligently left to the decision of Samiti.

3. Poverty Eradication Programme

Basically forest has been the major source of earning a livelihood among the tribals. Since the decay of forest and consequent lessoning of minor forest produce and the wild games, tribals have taken to peasantry as their primary source of earning. And the size of land in the tribal pockets is continuously decreasing. There has also been land erosion. There has been some migration among the tribals. The tribals traditionally are known for their immobility. Now they are perhaps the most mobile people. In search of jobs they migrate to the neighbouring states of Gujarat and Madhya Pradesh. All this has raised a crucial question. There is need to help the tribals to identify more and more local resources which could help them to generate income.

For the generation of income the government has introduced certain employment schemes. These schemes are within the power of Panchayat Samiti. The framers of Act have given options to the Samiti to implement one or more schemes for providing employment to the people. The Act has enumerated a few schemes which can be applied by the Samiti. The employment scheme includes Integrated Rural Development Programme (IRDP). Training of Rural Youth for Self-employment TRYSEM, and a few other schemes. It is with the Samiti to decide which programme would suit to its needs. The idea in launching the programmes is to eradicate poverty among the tribals. The tribals can generate new and additional income but they terribly lack in resources and technical know-how. The Act gives ample scope to the Samiti to push forward for such programmes which can give them opportunities of income generation.

There has emerged a contradiction of action among the tribals—particularly the women. They find their empowerment a very profound experience. They have reservation at all the three tiers of Panchayati Raj. But subjective consciousness hardly gives substantial money for improving the life style. In this respect the programmes of poverty eradication give a subjective boost but the end result fall in the realm of failure. But this has also to be verified from the field.

4. Common Needs of People

Food, clothes and shelter are the basic needs of the society. These needs fall within the jurisdiction of Panchayat. For instance, people should have some provisions for housing. Some assistance is always required to construct and repair the houses. There is also need for potable drinking water, fuel and sources of energy. The need for roads and particularly link roads cannot be over emphasised. Solar energy has to be produced locally. Flushout latrines have to be constructed. All these areas of common needs fall within the purview of Samiti. If there are no schemes regarding these needs from government, the Samiti can take initiative to raise some funds to fulfil the needs. Much depends on and resourcefulness of the Samiti members to facilitate the members. Decisions on this account required much of vision and farsightedness.

5. New Sources of Income

The Panchayat is given an option to take to some known traditional ways of earning money. The tribals have shifted from forest to farming. They are advised also to take to some occupations which are common to peasantry. Among these are included animal husbandry, poultry farming, dairy, piggery, fishery and things of this kind which are related to agriculture. If the tribals makes some dent in this new realm of occupation they can make some additional money. The Samiti is given option to move in this direction and encourage villagers to implement some of the schemes. Social forestry is another area which can help the people generate income. The Act has also covered a few new areas where the Samiti can make some headway. These field include cottage industries, village crafts, adult education, health programmes, development of women and children, handicapped people, and organisation of fairs and festivals. Vast areas of village life have been kept open for the Samiti to explore. The list of activities to be undertaken by the Samiti is very exhaustive. It would not be wrong to say that everything which is under the village sky has been left to Samiti for manipulation. No Samiti can venture to lay its hand on all these activities. What the Act has done, is to explore all possibilities of village development. The decisions are left to the discretion of the Samiti. And here lies the vision of Samiti. The Samiti should have its hands on the needs of the people and once these have been identified, the schemes can be manipulated according to grass-roots need and situations.

Zila Parishad: Structure and Function

Zila Parishad is the apex body of Panchayati Raj. In the former Panchayati Raj, members to the Zila Parishad were elected by the Pradhans of the Panchayat Samiti of a district. The elections to Zila Parishad was, therefore, indirect. The present Act seeks the mandate of the villagers to elect directly all the members of the Zila Parishad.

The rule of one-third part of members for women also applies for this apex body. The Act has contemplated a definite number of seats for women for the position of Zila Pramukh. This is stipulated through random method. For instance in tribal sub-plan area the position of Zila Pramukh goes to a tribal woman. In addition to the directly elected members of Zila Parishad, the MPs and MLAs are also invited to the meeting of Zila Parishad. However these invitees do not have right to vote. Normally the size of Zila Parishad members varies from 40 to 50.

One basic characteristic of Zila Parishad according to the present Act is that the total responsibility of executing and framing the development programmes rests with the Zila Parishad. Earlier the collector of the district wielded this power. Though the collector even today exercises his power, in all cases formal decisions are taken by the members of Zila Parishad. It is possible that the Collector may influence the decision of the Samiti but then he ceases to be a partner in decision-making.

The Act which gives power of decision-making to Zila Parishad is in the line of Panchayati Raj Act accepted by Maharashtra. It has its own advantages but if the Zila Parishad is weak in its wisdom, naturally the Collector uses his hegemonic power. The functions of Zila Parishad are varied and diverse. The Act has enumerated some 18 functions of Zila Parishad. The functions are elaborate and take within its purview all the realms of development life of the villagers. We have categorised them as below.

1. Agriculture, Horticulture and Irrigation

We have discussed it earlier that for the TSP area of Rajasthan agriculture is the prime occupation of people. The tribal peasantry by now has taken to settled agriculture. It may take to a large number of occupations such as government service, animal husbandry, poultry, fishing, entrepreneurship of the kind of provisional store, small contractorship, but agriculture remains the mainstay of earning a livelihood. It is this context of view that in TSP area the promotion of agriculture is the first priority of Panchayati Raj. With the limited size of land available with the tribals, the objective of Panchayati Raj is to encourage the villagers to take the three crops a year. They are also motivated to take to other occupations such as horticulture and agriculture related occupations such as processing of pulses, groundnut and so on. The Zila Parishad has agriculture and irrigation as areas of development. It can take up programmes for watershed management. Besides irrigation the Zila Parishad also promotes community pump sets as another means of irrigation.

2. Social Forestry

The traditional forest cover has largely been decayed. There is programme for aforestation. The aforestation can be developed through the idea of social forestry. According to it the forest is socially owned by the village community. In the development of social forestry the people are made accountable to the preservation and maintenance of social forestry.

3. Poultry and Dairy Farming

Our argument is that whatever development activities which are given to Zila Parishad are also put in the agenda of Panchayat Samiti. What is special about the schemes adopted by Zila Parishad is that the schemes are not directly implemented by it. Zila Parishad is never an executive body. Its involvement is at the level of planning and helping the Samiti for execution. The plans are first referred to Zila Parishad. Here these plans are discussed, analysed and are constituted in such a way that they are handed over to the Samiti.

4. Husbandry and Dairy Farming

It appears that with the increase in technology, the known agriculture implements would be lesser used in agricultural operations. Cattle therefore, have their restricted use of yielding milk to the community. We must mention here that in the TSP area neither Green Revolution has come, nor the White Revolution. If the people are given consciousness for development, it is possible to launch with the dairy farming in the TSP area. There is a great scope for development of dairy farming in south Rajasthan. It is interesting to note that out of the total need of milk in south Rajasthan, a part of it is received from Mehsana district of north Gujarat. White Revolution cannot be far behind, TSP has a huge scope for exploring the development of dairy farming in south Rajasthan. It is with this perspective in mind that the framers of Panchayati Raj, have put dairying as an agenda for Zila Parishad.

5. Fishing

The regions of south Rajasthan is rich for the development of fisheries. The tribals are traditionally quite adept in fisheries. They have been using indigenous nets for their catch. Small ponds and hilly rivers are always close to them. They are skilled in this art. With this occupational background in mind the Zila Parishad has been given scope to modernize fisheries. If proper decision are taken, that is, if members at Zila Parishad have some technical know-how about fisheries a great scope lies ahead in this field. However, a setback has come in the speedy development of fisheries in the region. A numerically strong group of tribals have accepted Bhagatism, that is, a puritanist cult of Hinduism which urges the tribals to abhor to take to drinking and non-vegetarian food. Aversion to non-vegetarianism—not even taking eggs is likely to discourage the Zila Parishad to take to fishing and poultry as a secondary source of income.

6. Infrastructure Facilities

If we look at the catalogue of functions of Zila Parishad along with Panchayat Samiti, we would immediately find that the items of development programme are the same. It is natural. The difference is at the level of planning and execution. The Zila Parishad takes all these programmes for discussion and finalises them in terms of the availability of funds. It is the Zila Parishad which decides the priorities for programmes bracketing then with the availability of funds and the sense of social justice in the allocation of programmes. It is possible that the Zila Parishad could initiate a programme in those Samities only which are weakest of weak and the weak are given the next chance. As a matter of fact the prime function of Zila Parishad is to make its decision judiciously and heavily oriented to social justice. For instance there are funds for the management of potable water in the district. In this situation the Zila Parishad has to identify the Panchayat Samities and their cluster of villages highly starved of water as compared to other villages which are not so badly off. This kind of judicious discrimination has to be taken by Zila Parishad. Our argument is that despite the development activities being recurrent and repetitive the role of Zila Parishad is to take decision. The emphasis here is on decision. The emphasis here is on social justice. The emphasis here is to identify the weakest among the weak and this very aptly differentiates the functioning of Zila Parishad from the Panchayat Samiti.

The Panchayat Samiti has all the functions or items of development activities which are assigned to Zila Parishad. But here the emphasis is different. Panchayat Samiti executes the programme. It makes decisions within the permitted alternatives provided by the Zila Parishad. For instance the Zila Parishad gives a funds for upgrading, say two middle schools in the Samiti. True, the Samiti would execute the programme but would also decide to allocate the schools to particular villages. Thus the decisions about the execution of programmes partly lies with the Samiti but its major function is to bring to ground the programmes given to it by the Zila Parishad. Thus despite the items of development being the same there is difference of emphasis and degree between the two tiers of Panchayati Raj.

7. Health and Hygiene

Medical care of mother and child is a new perspective given by W.H.O. as a part of family welfare. This falls in the development programmes of Zila Parishad. In close relation to health and hygiene is the sustainability of village environment. The Zila Parishad looks after this aspect of community life. As the membership of Parishad has a wide spectrum comprising all the villages of district, common programmes of health and hygiene and environment can be attended by Zila Parishad. Take for instance the programme of Pulse Polio or Malaria eradication. These programmes are inclusive of the whole district and Zila Parishad is best suited to uniformally implement these programmes.

8. Weaker Sections: Welfare Programme and Social Reforms

The TSP area has the basic objective of helping the tribals to rise above from poverty line. For poverty removal there are a large number of programmes. It is required to identify the poor. It is also obligatory for Zila Parishad to mobilize the subaltern groups of the whole district. Such a mobilisation can be made for the whole district. Similarly the senior citizens, widows and handicapped persons could also be identify at the macro level of the district. These are some of the welfare activities which are put within the purviews of Zila Parishad. In some of the cases, therefore, the Parishad also works as an executive body.

Tribal Women

Panchayati Raj is a very comprehensive category. It includes all that which goes in the name of villages. The three tiers of the Panchayati Raj constitute its body. The role of women at all the three tiers is significant. We need to explain the significance with same elaboration. Women are discriminated against males. In literate and progressive society also the discrimination goes on. But the nature and content of discrimination at the village level is much different from urban level. In urban society, if we leave out the exceptional cases of bride burning which is found among high caste Hindus, women residing in rural communities have to suffer the most. In urban communities, the women are literate, they have social connections and they can easily move the court. But in the tribal society only the rule of thumb, and mostly the muscle powers works popularly. They are easily made victims of beating and violence. Women do not have alternatives of economic support. And when they are showed the door by the males, the rest is a chaos in their life. In such a society the reservation in Panchayati Raj at all the three tiers, even if nothing happen substantially, does give a sign of relief to the tribal women. Subjectively they have a statutory position in the Panchayat Samiti. She has some kind of nexus with the political leaders and officials. A little swing on their part, they can defeat a confidence motion. Economically it does not give any benefit but in formal terms they are important members. And it is here that the significance of women reservation lies in the Panchayat Acts.

The chapter that follows will discuss the socio-economic position of women in terms of our sample group.

CHAPTER 6

The Canvas

We have contacted women informants along with men informants in the field. The informants do not reside in vacuum. They have their connections; they have their networks, they have their background. Their perception of rural society is according to their age, caste, education, gender, occupation and political orientation. Their cognition about the surrounding universe is very important. The empowerment given to them by statutory provisions is interpreted by their cognition. Before we discuss the empowerment in its wider dimensions — social and cultural, we would prepare a canvas which will help us to bring out the picture.

Methodological Strategy

Our sample group consists of four districts and four Panchayat Samities. We have not taken up any particular district for our intensive study. The main target of our study is Tribal Sub-Plan Area. From this area we have drawn out a sample of 100 respondents notwithstanding any particular Panchayat Samiti or district. Out of this sample purposively we have taken 70 females and 30 males. The number of female respondents exceeds the males. This we have done to highlight the issue of women empowerment. The canvas on a broader plan shows that the female illiteracy is lower than the female literacy found at the state and national level. Another important thing about the canvas is that the life in the plains has never been comfortable. Both for tribal male and female, traditionally, the Bhils have been residing in hills and forests. In south Rajasthan such a region is called *Pal*. *Pal* is a concept which indicates specific hilly and forest region differentiated from the plain's region. *Pal* is also a cultural region. Anyone who lives in the *Pal* has a distinct culture from the plain region. It is because of this cultural differentiation that normally the Bhils residing in *Pals* do not have matrimonial relations with the Bhils of the plains. While the *Pal* Bhils are known as *Palvee* Bhils, the plain Bhils are called *Chokhyar* Bhils. The *Chokhyar* Bhils are much Hinduised compared to *Palvee* Bhils. Though reservation in services and availability of jobs in different *Pals* have minimised the differences between these two territorial specificities, the identity of a Bhil is recognised through his *Pal* or plains.

In course of time the *Palvee* Bhils also migrated to plains. This migration has now almost become exodus. Everyone wants to run towards tehsil, town and district headquarters in search of jobs. The Bhils are not an exception. A Bhil when in the forest can very boldly encounter a panther, but scared very much when he is in the city or when he is in a government office. Whenever the government that is the Patwari or a police constable made his presence in the villages, the first action of the Bhil would be to climb on the hillock instructing his family to convey that he was not available. This is the force of the canvas that when the Bhil women comes to attend the Panchayat Samiti meeting she is not in her usual bearings. In close contact with the Panchayat Samiti members which also include non-tribals, she is more than scared.

I.P. Desai who has worked among the *Halpatis*, a tribal group of south Gujarat says that the Tribals have yet another reason to be scared of non-tribal groups. The *Sahookars* the traders who have always been high caste Hindus have exploited the tribals. Though the *Sahookars* advance loan but they are first rate cheaters. When there is a meeting of the tribals, normally they do not allow non-tribals to participate in the meeting. The statement of I.P. Desai runs:[1]

> The Adivasis knew the non-Adivasis through the exploiters only, namely the moneylenders, the police and other government officers and liquor shop owners. They, therefore, distrusted all non-Adivasis. They did not want any 'outsider' to be present at their meetings and made a rule that if any 'outsider' came to the meeting the proceeding should stop. The outsiders were actually the exploiter primarily. The 'Ujalick' was disliked because he was an exploiter first and non-Adivasi next.

The situation described by I.P. Desai about the *Halpaties* of south Gujarat is not without its parallel in south Rajasthan. Whether a person is a Jain, Bania or Rajput caste or any other castes is a first rate exploiter of the tribals. In such a situation it is very difficult for a tribal woman who has been bestowed by statutory empowerment would be able to minimise her discrimination to some extent. Women are normally surrounded by males — tribal and non-tribal and what is worse they observed *Purdah*. They cannot see eye to eye with men. These aspects of our canvas are important to comprehend the social reality of TSP area.

It would not be out of place that when the Seventy-Third Amendment was put in the parliament it was hoped and it was desired that in course of time, the tribal women would acquire the prerequisite of reading, writing and arithmetic. It should also be mentioned that there is much difference in literacy and education. If the tribal women are literate though we are afraid, it would not empower them. Our guess is that to translate the empowerment into stark reality, good education is required. We have passed fifty years after independence without making primary education compulsory in tribal area, do we hope to have new generation of tribals coming out of the portals of colleges and universities? The question is relevant but we will be able to discuss it in the next chapter when we have the empirical data at our command.

Respondents Age

Age is a great determining factor in taking decisions. The assessment of maturity of a person varies from society to society. Among the tribals when a man is able to plough with his own hands, cut the forestry or work on stone independently, he is judged to be mature. This warrants his marriage also. The age in this situation is fifteen years and more. A female is considered to be mature when she can fetch water from the *nallah*, grind corn and clean the cattleshed. She can now be married; she is mature. On the other hand after attaining forty years the men begin to look quite fragile. He appears to an old age. This kind of variation in the perception of age must be granted when we look at the age groups of 100 respondents.

Table 6.1 which we give below shows that more than half of the respondents fall in the age group of 18 to 35. This is the younger age and it is expected that this age group would work energetically for rural development. About one-fourth of the informants fall in the category of middle age group—36 - 45. Those above the middle age group constitute one-fifth of the total strength of the informants. Only 5 per cent have attained an age of 60 and above. The age group analysis is quite promising. Youngsters have a major role. They are joined by middle aged respondents. Interestingly enough only 5 per cent could be called old people. The details of data are given in Table 6.1.

Table 6.1
Respondent's Age Groups

Age Group	*Frequency*	*Percentage*
18 - 25	26	26%
26 - 35	25	25%
36 - 45	24	24%
46 - 60	20	20%
60 and above	05	05%
Total	100	100%

Social Formation

It should not be assumed that every second person in TSP area is a tribal. In Dungarpur and Banswara the tribal population does not exceed 70 per cent. In Udaipur the percentage even goes down. Thus in all the three tiers of Panchayati Raj there are other backward classes and high caste Hindus besides the tribal members. The data generated by us in the field shows that a high percentage of members belong to scheduled tribes followed by scheduled castes. Other backward classes are lesser than the caste Hindu members. It indicates that the tribals carry a hegemonic power with them. They can decide matters in their favour. But the OBC and caste Hindus have a strength of 20 members and they in collaboration with scheduled caste can make a difference. While discussing the Panchyati Raj institutions we must mention that the category of tribals is altogether different from the scheduled caste category. The scheduled castes suffer from disabilities which relate to untouchability. There is no such disability with the scheduled tribe. In most of the cases the high caste Hindus accept food from the hands of scheduled tribes. Smoke is very easily exchanged. In such a situation there is always a possibility of scheduled caste shifting towards high caste Hindus. They have an organic association with them. The scheduled tribes are in no case considered to be Hindus. They are backwards who have recently come out of hills and forests. Organically they have no links with scheduled castes and OBCs. The data generated from the field are presented in Table 6.2.

Table 6.2
Social Formation in Panchayati Raj

Kind of Social Formation	*Frequency*	*Percentage*
Scheduled Tribes	68	68%
Scheduled Castes	12	12%
Other Backward Classes	09	09%
High Caste Hindus	11	11%
Total	100	100

Educational Profile

Recent discussion on education has stressed the point that many of our key problems relate to the absence of education. Our population growth is largely due to non-existence of education among the tribals. We have mentioned it earlier that the states which have taken to female education have made considerable scores in reducing the population growth. There is no specific data on the growth of population among the tribals. But we have data from district level. True, polygamy has declined substantially in the tribal areas. It is believed that if, women education is promoted among the tribals, the population growth, infant mortality and maternal mortality will be reduced in a large way. The empowerment status would also be translated in a better way. Providing such a canvas we now read out our data on education.

Table 6.3
Educational Status

Status	*Frequency*	*Percentage*
Illiterate	07	07%
Literate and Pre-primary	22	22%
Primary to Middle Standard	23	23%
Secondary and Senior Secondary Standard	21	21%
Under-graduate	18	18%
Postgraduate	06	06%
Professional and Technical	03	03%
Total	100	100

The data about education includes both males and females. On a broader plane it can be argued that a little less than half the respondents have education from pre-primary level to middle standard. One very interesting feature is that a little less than one-fourth of respondents are closed to secondary and higher secondary level. There is negligible number of postgraduates and professionals. The data are not much disheartening. On a broader plane the TSP area has a rich network of secondary and senior secondary schools. There are colleges also at the district headquarters. Our observations shows that the college unions at Dungarpur, Banswara and Pratapgarh are dominated by tribal students. The colleges have much politicised the tribal students. If they joined the Panchayati Raj institution, the future would be bright indeed.

Occupational Orientation

Occupation is the prime mover. We enquired about the ways about earning a livelihood to the respondents. It is interesting to mention here that the ways of generating income among the tribals are varying. At the national level the data given by Project of India (POI) are very interesting. It is found that a large number of tribals in the country are giving up their traditional occupations. For instance hunting, gathering forest produce and other forest related occupation are declining. It is because of the ecological degradation. On the other hand, new occupations such as horticulture and sericulture are fast appearing. A marked shift in the occupational structure of tribals such as seen at occupational level.

In the case of our area of enquiry though there is no such a shift available, surely agriculture has been made quite intensive. In the parts of Banswara and Chittorgarh districts canal irrigation is available. Earlier the tribals took agriculture only during wet and dry weather but now *Mahi* and *Jakham* dams have enabled the tribals to take three crops a year. The cropping pattern has witnessed a sharp change. More and more commercial crops are taken. This has considerably influenced the consumption level of the people. Data collected by us on this account reveal that 70 per cent of respondents have their own land and they cultivate themselves. The land size varies between six and thirteen *bighas*. The land in the terrain of TSP area is normally fertile. All the respondents take to wet weather crops namely maize and pulses. However, during the dry weather season commercial crops are taken. The surpluses are taken to market and whatever is produced during the third crop in summer is exclusively meant for market. The surplus crops bring home cash money. It is this part of yield which determines life style of the people. It is interesting to find that women work very skilfully in irrigation activities. The third crop which is horticulture including the cultivation of vegetables is marketed mostly by women. A visitor to Pratapgarh and Banswara city found that tribal women make a vegetable market which traces its origin only in the recent past. Women have developed a 'wisdom' which has experienced them to make transactions with the retailer in the vegetable selling. The bargain has proved to be profitable for the tribals. It would be an exception to find a male vegetable retailer in this market. Similar markets have emerged in the towns of Simalwara and Jadol. Vegetables which were normally non-existent in towns within tribal setting have emerged conspicuously. The market owes much to tribal women.

The data further shows that those who do not own much land, resort to agricultural labour. Another outlet for working as labourer is in the field of construction works or work in forest area. We have not much frequencies or percentages in other occupations but it must be observed that a new beginning has been made in the emergence of new occupations. Service in government departments, NGOs and private sector are the new employers. Despite the low percentage in this field, the area has been opened to the tribals. The data are given below.

Table 6.4
Occupational Calling: New Areas of Employment

Occupation	*Frequency*	*Percentage*
Agriculture	70	70%
Agricultural Labour	20	20%
Services in Other Sectors	06	06%
Horticulture	04	04%
Total	100	100

Yearly Earnings

The government of Rajasthan has fixed minimum wages for the labourers, it being Rs. 60 per day but normally work in the tribal hinterland is not paid according to this Act. Normally it is the market which determines the rates. At the level of surplus production in the field the tribals of TSP area grow wheat during dry weather. The rates of wheat are competitive. So are the rates of vegetables. Those of the tribals who are engaged in government service get an envious monthly pocket. Taking into consideration all this aspects of wage payment we find that 28 per cent of informants fall in the income brackets that is (10,000). Still a larger number of informants namely, 40 per cent belong to the category of (20,000 - 30,000). About one-fourth of the respondents belong to the income bracket of (31,000 to 40,000). When we go higher in the income scale naturally the percentage scores go down. The data are given in Table 6.5.

Table 6.5

Categories of Income	*Percentage*
10,000 — 20,000	23%
20,000 — 30,000	40%
30,000 — 40,000	30%
40,000 — 50,000	04%
50,000 and above	03%
	100%

If we combine the total economic structure of the tribals it could be safely said that the people are deprived many of their traditional income assets. The data which we have from anthropological ethnography and the gazetteers inform us that it did not cost a tribal anything in cash money when he erected his hutment. He took all the wood from the forest. And he was permitted to do it. His plough and cart was also made from the forest wood. What he had to part with from his side was only labour. Now since the forest became unfriendly to him due to the revised forest laws, the Bhil cultivator is obliged to purchase material for constructing the house in the timber shops of the city. His traditional privileges have now been monetised. It is in this context that we have to look to the tribal economic problems and the premises within which the female members have to operate in the Panchayat Samiti. It appears that the tribal women have to encounter a new situation which is unconventional and unhistorical for them. We had frequent and protracted stay in the Tribal Sub-Plan Area and we found that during the off weather months women and children are found engaged in collecting fuel wood. Perhaps it is the job of the women to arrange for the day-to-day needs of fuel etc. for the people. This is a problem which we hope constitute a running theme for the issues presented in the Panchayat Samiti meetings. What happens to it, does the issue emerge in meeting, we shall examine it at the later stage.

Marriage and Family Status

Marriage among tribals is a contract. Any of the spouses can decide to dissolve the marriage. The only disputed part of marriage dissolution is the bride price. This too is settled between the two parties and sometime with the involvement through the traditional Panchayat. The status of women as discussed early is not inferior as is found among the caste Hindus. In matriarchal society as Tiplut Nongbri informs the status of women is quite very high. The Bhil women enjoys better status in the community. Out of our sample group of hundred informants the women constitute 70, the remaining being males. The data which we have generated shows in simple figures that 83 informants are married and 17 unmarried. All the female informants are married. But what we find behind the figure is very interesting. We asked a women member of Panchayat Samiti: What do you want to do which would be for the welfare of women? The answer was straightforward. She discussed with me the problems of tribal women who reside in the villages situated along the national highway which links Bombay and Delhi. She says that a few of the women have taken to immoral sex relations. They serve the truck drivers during night who passed through the roads. The transactions are attractive. According to her estimate it comes something between 150 to 200 rupees per night. Whatever may be the moral turpitude of immoral traffic, what is nationally important is that it gives rise to sexually transmitted diseases and still worst HIV positive. Finally she summed up her answer by saying: there is a worse erosion of sex, can the Panchayat Samiti intervene in the matter. Does it come within the provision of the Panchayat Act? It shows that despite being an unlettered tribal women they have a concern for the cause of the society. Another issue which is related to marital status and family is of population growth. She has no perfect understanding about the techniques of limiting the size of a family. Does it require an awareness programme to make the tribal women familiar about the national needs of the country.

The members were subjected to inform about the number of children that they have in their family. Our precise question was to know about family size. It is interesting to know that 28 per cent of informants stand for family size of 3-5 children. Following it, 22 per cent have a family size between 5-7 children. Only a meagre number that is 4 per cent have a real large family consisting of 7 and above children. However a redeeming aspect of responses is that 6 to 18 per cent of informants stand for a family of 1 - 2 children. The Act disqualifies a man to stand for Panchayat membership if he has children exceeding two. It appears that such a sanction would go a long way in limiting the family size of tribal rural society. But the situation as we find today is a great satisfaction. Traditionally the tribals have been notorious to have large families. In one of the proverbial folk songs of the Bhils of Panchmahals of Gujarat, it is said that a Bhil named Nanaji Damore had twelve wives. He was all the time tormented by one wife or the other. For instance, the folk song goes, a bald wife wanted a comb from Ahmedabad; the wife who was blind put the desire for a pair of goggles. The folk song vividly shows the polygamous status of tribal society. Greater the polygamy, more the children. At least this tradition has become today a thing of the past. The data generated on account of family size are given below.

Table 6.6

Size of the Family		*Frequency*
0 — 1		06
1 — 2		18
3 — 4		22
5 — 6		28
7 — 8		22
8 and above		04
	Total	100

ELECTION PROCEDURE: INVOLVEMENT IN ELECTIONING

Elections of any kind assume understanding of the processing of nomination, withdrawal, electioneering and getting support of the voters. In Panchayati Raj the whole process is performed at local level. The involvement of the people, therefore, is quite expected as they are on the spot. Contesting elections for what? The question presupposes powers and duties of elected members. In our sample group there were persons who contested elections and involved themselves in the whole processes. We have generated first hand data from the candidates involved. We will here discuss the whole electioneering processes in its major parts.

Nomination

There is an air of contesting election. One gets motivated or insensitive to contest the election. We enquired about the motivating agencies who obliged the candidate to stand for a particular position. The major motivation (34 per cent) comes from party workers. Parties in this election after Seventy-Third Amendment were in dilemma. One-third of seats were reserved for women and it was difficult for them to get suitable candidates for the same. Our field experience tells us vividly that women in the field normally were not aware about their reservation. We know the party leaders had to run from post to pillar to find out a suitable woman candidate. There were several cases we saw that women were chased by the party workers. One woman candidate had gone to clean her clothes at the local *nalah*. The political worker had to go there and having found that she had left the *nalah* she was found way back in the neighbourhood. She refused to know anything about election and expressed her inability to involve herself in the run. In this situation influentials and kinsmen were summoned. And at last long the party succeeded in getting the consent of the woman. In another case a woman very flatly refused:

> Panchayats are bad. There are much of quarrels. I do not want to drag myself into this mess.

She could not be influenced to put her signature on the nomination form. We could hardly find five women who had their own desire to contest elections. Next to the motivation of party workers is the persuasion received from the kin members. Among the tribals kinship ties are the determining ties. Anthropologists display enough ethnographical data to bring home the fact that in a tribal group there is no influential factor to motivate a man. Data on Gonds and Bhils show that if you want to get a work done in tribal societies establish yourself as one of the relatives. In all cases among the tribals, blood is always thicker than water. In filling the nomination form for an office there are other factors also. For instance family members have a great role in pursuing a man to contest an election. 18 per cent of informants were influenced by family members. There is also influence of the office bearers of Panchayati Raj. The details about the factors influencing nomination to election are given in Table 6.7.

Table 6.7
Factors of Motivation and Incentives in Filling up Nominations

Influencing Agency	*Frequency*	*Percentage*
1. Family members	18	18%
2. Kinsmen	19	19%
3. Tribal Community	17	17%
4. Panchayat Officials such as Panch, Sarpanchas, Pradhan and M.L.A.	08	08%
5. Party Workers	24	24%
6. N.G.Os.	10	10%
7. Candidates own desire	04	04%
Total	100	100%

Election Campaign

There is no fanfare in tribal area for election campaign. But such a kind of statement is simplistic. True, at the level of Ward Panch there is almost no competition. There are cases which shows that in some instances even no candidates comes forward for filling the nomination forms. Here the role of election campaign is almost non-existent. At this level the candidate contest elections in his individual capacity and the role of party forum is denied, constitutionally. Theoretically at ward Panch level elections are free from party politics.

The real election begins at the Panchayat Samiti level. Here the election is for the members of Panchayat Samiti. In a single Panchayat there are wards. It is all calculated on population basis. In some cases if the villages are small they could number five to ten. Here the competition is intense and the candidate is required to tour all the wards. Jeeps are used, pamphlets and hand bills are brought out. The general enthusiasm which marks any election in the country can be seen in a miniature form in the election of Panchayat Samiti members. At the Zila Parishad level the area of operation becomes more wider. In a district say Udaipur there are eleven Panchayat Samities. Panchayat Samities are divided into wards for Zila Parishad membership. The candidate makes a wider coverage for electioneering. In this case also expenses of election campaign get multiplied. It is said that normally in the elections of Panchayat Samiti and Zila Parishad a candidate has to spend approximately something between 1 lakh to 3 lakhs. However, at the ward level no substantial amount is spent.

The elections at the Panchayat Samiti and Zila Parishad are being taken as defeat or victory of a particular political party. In such a situation electioneering is taken up by political parties. There is much involvement of the candidate and party at this level of election.

The elections in Panchayati Raj have in some cases cut across the family and kinship ties. Normally as mentioned by us earlier tribal society is very deliberately interwoven by family and kinship ties. But the elections have enthused people to such an extent that they have crossed the border line of family. In one case the husband got defeated in an election and in another the wife became victorious. In some cases both husband and wife got elected to the position of Sarpanch. We return to our discussion on election campaign. Leaving aside the Ward Panch election, in other forms of election the candidates approach the voter on individual basis, they go from door-to-door.

Data generated in this respect show that more than half of the candidates have the approach to the voters through door to door canvassing. Followed by it in 56 per cent cases electioneering is done by party workers. Even the party possess of the rank of members of Legislative Assembly and Deputy Ministers and leaders of State party also participate in Panchayat Samiti and Zila Parishad elections. There is yet another approach to the voters through written appeals. One very important feature which has worked in a clandestine way to offer local hard drinks to the voters. This tactics which works in city urban areas also works successfully in the interior parts of the tribal areas. The details of data are given in Table 6.8.

Table 6.8
Modes of Election Campaign: Panchayat Samiti and Zila Parishad Levels

Kind of Election Campaign	*Frequency*
1. Door-to-door Campaign	68
2. Caste Panchayat and Workers	44
3. Party Bosses	56
4. Party Workers	56
5. Group Meetings	33
6. Appeals and Hand Bills	41
7. Advertisement in Local Newspapers	08
8. Foul incentives of liquor, cash or money and mutton	41 .

Election Results: Unanimous and Contest

Elections in a democracy indicate the spirit of participating in nation building. Panchayati Raj is the grass-root forum of participating democracy. We are looking for the spirit of contesting elections with all enthusiasm at village level. True, in part Panchayati Raj Institutions were kept away from party politics. They were not contested in party name. And if a candidate was returned uncontested, the village was given a special grant for development considering that the village has shown its traditional unity. Village unity has remained a long time myth in rural India. But in the present context when a number of political and social factors are working in a village life, the traditional unity is cut across on ethnic, caste, and factional rivalries.

In TSP area there have been some cases of unanimous elections. The reason for uncontested elections has been lack of interest in standing for an office. Our data on this account show that in our sample group there are 17 informants who have succeeded in coming to office uncontested. These uncontested candidates were not interested in the elections but were persuaded to fill the nomination and since there were no other rivals, they were returned uncontested. In their conversation, it became clear that even after getting the position they were not enthusiastic to work in the Committee. One of them responded:

> I do not know what I am expected to do. I was caught unawares. I put the signature and look here I am in the Panchayati Raj.

Unanimous elections under the provisions of Act show that the people at the grass-root level are not keen to work for Panchayati Raj. Such candidates do not fulfil any prerequisite expectations of a candidate. They are simply in position.

Formal Role of Political Parties

Surely elections in Panchayati Raj are contested on the basis of party membership. But there is a strange situation in Panchayati Raj election. Membership to party is actually post-election phenomenon. It is after election that the candidates are identified with the party. In our sample group 23 per cent of informants have opted for a particular party after they were returned successful in the election. Hypothetically, if they had been defeated, there would not be any mention of party for such candidate.

However, in the TSP area out of our sample group 53 per cent belong to Congress, 38 per cent BJP, 5 per cent Janata Dal and CPM (male) 4 per cent. The TSP area has a special political identity. Mama Baleshwar Dayal of Banswara was considered to be the god father by the tribals. He started with socialist orientation in the background of Ram Manohar Lohia. Gradually his influence got eroded. He became follower of Janata Dal. The CPM (male) group has his pocket of influence in Dungarpur. But above all Congress party seems to have its influence in the two districts of Dungarpur and Banswara. The political behaviour of our sample group has to be judged from this historical backdrop.

Election Expenditure

To bring out any precise figure for expenditure on Panchayati Raj election is very difficult. The expenses increase with the increase in electorate. At the Gram Panchayat level there are wards only and what is worse, normally the villagers lack enthusiasm for contesting as Ward Panchas. Competition being non-existent at this level, there is hardly any expenditure. But in the Panchayat Samiti and Zila Parishad the respective jurisdiction extend and this involves expenditure on touring the area. People are also appeased by the provision of other incentives and in some cases money also. 'The faction leaders are normally paid some amount'. At the Zila Parishad level the expenditure multiplies. We have generated some data which show the amount spent on contesting election.

Table 6.9
Estimated Amount Spent on Election

Amount	*Frequency*	*Percentage*
Below 1,000	05	05%
1001— 5,000	25	25%
5,000 — 10,000	29	29%
10,000 — 20,000	11	11%
20,000 — 30,000	07	07%
30,000 — 40,000		
40,000 — 50,000	04	04%
50,000 and above	03	03%
Total	100	

Our interviews with the Zila Pramukh show that an exaggerated amount is spent for Zila Pramukh in all cases it comes to more than 1 lakh rupees. I asked a very nice question to a member elected to Zila Pramukh. What is it that you spent so much of money for this post? As the question was nice, the answer too was equally very simple: "it is all for the service of my village people." Nobody would be satisfied to learn that rupees 1 lakh are spend for serving the people. Service to people does not require spending of money. The fact of the matter is that the money spent is the money put to investment. If in the election of a female candidate or a male candidate constitute such a big amount it has certain wider implications. There is rampant corruption in the management of local funds and subsidies at the Panchayat Samiti level. These amounts are misappropriated and misused. There are various sources which indicate that in the Panchayati Raj much of the public money is misused. Such a logic might partly explain the expenditure made on election. When the money spent is on the election of women, obviously its management has been made by the supporting males, surely her husband. In such a situation the autonomous status of the women candidate is jeopardised. She remains a proxy member. There is a biblical saying: "One who pays for the piper calls for the tune." She has only to respond to the tune which the investors desire.

Free and Fair Elections: A Myth

It is very popular in politics to talk about free and fair elections. Right from National Election Commission to the State Election Commission it is reiterated that the elections are conducted on democratic and judicious principles. So far Panchayat elections are concerned, free and fair elections idiom is myth rather than fact, is a fiction rather than reality. The things are managed in such a way that overnight the whole election scenario gets transformed. There are fake voters. There is fake voting and above all the lower sections are threatened to go to polling booth for voting. In such a situation conducting of elections on fair lines become very much difficult. The factional rivalry is so pervasive in rural country that it is difficult for an ordinary man to exercise his vote. In the Panchayati Raj election there is greater possibility of election irregularities, violence and fraud compared to general elections. It must also be said that if a party happens to be in power it can successfully manage to suppress news of violence and irregularities. In our sample group some cases of violence have been recorded. Though nobody comes openly to challenge the functioning of elections, it becomes a common talk of the village that all sorts of irregularities occur to get a candidate elected. There are some very strange coincidences also. In Salumber Panchayat Samiti of Udaipur district wives of the three Panchayati Raj members—Sarpanch, Up-sarpanch and ward panch got elected. It is nothing short of conspiracy that how such comedies happen.

In all, in the recent Panchayati Raj elections in Rajasthan (February 2000) several incidences of violence has occurred. Violence is very uncommon in Rajasthan and at the village level it is generally unheard of. Despite this the violent situations indicate that the political parties have played games in foul way. The cases of repolling have been ordered in such situations in the state.

Counting of Votes

The rural people have now taken interest in the counting of votes. They are very keen to see their candidate returned. On the day of counting people come in crowds to throng the place of voting. We asked respondents about their interest in vote counting. It is found that both males and females are equally interested in vote counting. 35 per cent of both the sexes have agreed to look at the vote counting. Those who respond negatively, females outnumber the males.

Election Results

In Panchayati Raj all the steps of electioneering takes place locally. And therefore, there is a direct involvement of village people. Responding to the question that how did the people come to know about the election results, it is found that most of the people came to know about it through the announcement made by the returning officers. Result is also known through party workers (35 per cent) and family male members (30 per cent). The data are given in Table 6.10.

Table 6.10
Election Results

Agency Which Give the Result	*Frequency*			*Percentage*
	M	*F*	*Total*	
1. Announcement Made by Returning Officers	27	07	34	35%
2. Party Workers	02	28	30	30%
3. Family Male Members	—	30	30	30%
4. Through Village Gossips	01	05	06	05%
	30	70	100	100%

Concluding Observations

Empowerment studies have become household word. Even studies on women have also become very popular. It is believed that if women are given power they would rise on par with men. The whole gender problem which has become much pronounced in Europe and USA has also come to India. The nature of problem at both the places is different. In the Western countries women are highly educated. They stand neck to neck in fields of education, technology and management with men. In our country the hiatus is very wide. There are millions of women in the rural country who live below poverty line. Though they work in the field they are not economically independent. However, in urban India the elites and the high caste women have a different problem. What we argue is that women all over India are not homogenous. They differ in thin canvas.

We have made an effort to give a special profile of women in terms of their age, group, caste orientation and economic status. The objective has been to generate data on the socio-economic characteristics of the women in TSP area. Our understanding of tribal women is that there are some discriminations between men and women. These discriminations are institutional. However, it must be observed that the gender problem with the tribal women is not as serious as is found among the caste Hindu women residing in urban areas. In the next chapter we shall have occasion to analyse the cognition level of women about their surrounding world.

Reference

1. Desai, I.P., 'The Wedchhi Movement', in *History of Rural Development in Modern India*, New Delhi, 1977, p. 52.

CHAPTER 7

Levels of Cognition: The World View of Tribal Women

Methodologically, we contest abstract empiricism our argument is that the social reality has to be comprehended in its contextuality. The empowerment of women of the tribals has a history. No development programme can overlook or neglect history. Before launching a programme we must be familiar about the gender relations in the tribal area. We have stressed it earlier and we reiterate that tribal women are different from non-tribal women. The planners and the framers of Panchayati Raj should have kept this history of tribal society in mind. We propose here about the awareness of tribal women in terms of the rights granted to them. It is not for the first time that the tribals are given certain privileges. Right from the promulgation of India's Constitution we have given certain developmental and protective safeguards to women. About half a century has gone and the tribals have not attained a development stage, which could qualify them to improve their life style. Why?

It was envisaged in the Constitution that all source of development programmes should be introduced in the tribal areas. And this was done. We have floated eight five year plans and special tribal development programmes to uplift the standard of living. As desired by the Constitution every year the Commissioner of Scheduled Castes and Scheduled Tribes puts its progress report on the Floor of the House. It is only the other day that the Parliament has decided to extend the period of reservation for another ten years, that is, till 2010. Such a situation raised a large number of questions. The fact is that some of the tribals have attained the desired standard of life, but they are not descheduled. And interestingly those groups which were previously excluded from the scheduled lists of the tribals, have found their place in the list. Every day new list has been added for other backward classes. In any developing society such a situation is chaotic. There is something wrong somewhere. It appears that either the framers of Constitution were weak in their wisdom or the whole implementation of development programme was faulty and biased. What we find today and is supported by empirical studies is that most of the benefits of development programmes have been cornered by the elites the rich belonging into the tribal community. The masses of the people all through this long history have remained neglected. Our argument is that if we do not take the empowerment provisions carefully and if they do not fit with the historical contextuality of the women of this region, the empowerment scheme for which the government pats itself on its back would fall flat and would meet the same fate as our development programmes. The understanding of women about the empowerment should be clear. And it is here that the rub lies.

Movement: A Historical Failure

The history of the tribal development in south Rajasthan has several lessons. Perhaps our planners, political workers and developmental administrators have not taken any lessons from south Rajasthan tribal history. Let us go back to the first quarter of twentieth century. In south Rajasthan there was a tribal movement headed by Govind Giri. Govind Giri was not a Bhil by himself nor did he belong to any tribal group of south Rajasthan nor Panchmahals of Gujarat. The point is that he was not a son of a tribal. He was a *Banjara* — a nomadic. He started a movement which is known is *Bhagat Movement*. The Bhils of his time were more or less savages. They used to take beef meat. They committed highway robbery. They did not take agriculture as a settled way of life. Looking to all this state of life, very rightly Govind Giri wanted to convert Bhils to Hinduism. He advised them to wear *Jenav*, give up beef eating. They were also asked to abhor liquor and live a respectable life. The Bhagat movement took a momentum in the contiguous area of Rajasthan, Madhya Pradesh and Gujarat. Mangad is a small hill on the borders of Banswara district and Sunthrampur (Panchmahals) of Gujarat. Bhils were asked to assemble at Mangad. Govind Giri's movement was given a twist and the demand was put that the region of Panchmahals and the former princely states of Dungarpur and Banswara belonged to the Bhils. And Bhils should be allowed autonomy of this region. The Princely rulers controlled the movement. Shooting was resorted to and Govind Girl was sent to jail.

All in all if the Bhils of south Rajasthan committed any revolution, it was an ethnic revolution. Let us look back to history again. The Bhils were exploited but never did they give any rise to upheaval. They have been bearing all the discriminations and injustices without any clamour.

The Bhils are not prone to rise in revolt. Surely, they can make certain protest, they would strike and run back to forest openly, they would never encounter the situation. In such a historical set up, in 1959 the decentralised Panchayati Raj was given by Mohan Lal Sukhadia, the then Chief Minister of Rajasthan. It was 'heroic' on his part. But it was again a weakness of wisdom. Decentralisation was good. But he faltered. He gave it to a community who had a feudal mindset. The people could not respond adequately to Panchayati Raj. Our fear is that for launching a new scheme of the kind of empowerment there are certain social and cultural prerequisite. Are the women educationally, culturally and economically well equipped to respond to empowerment?

The New Forces

But in the changed time there is a ray of hope for the empowerment statute. The tribals including their women are also fast changing. There is a spread of education. More and more women are taking to vocational and professional courses. A large number of volunteers are working in the field. More and more scheduled tribe members are leaving their homes for industrial cities. When the members of the migrant groups reach their parent groups they are vibrant with the new culture which they have lived in urban centres. The new kind of gender relations which characterised the urban industrial country are also brought to the rural tribal society. Obviously this is not a planned change. It is all unplanned. This new wave of market hegemony, democratisation and education along with new technology has affected the tribals also. The tribal women are no exception. They have also taken kindly to this new change.

V.S. Naipaul has taken a stock of the social situation prevailing in India. He travels east, west, north and south of India. He makes his observation at the concluding part of his book: *India— A Million Mutinies Now* (1990). He observes:

> In the one hundred and thirty years or so since the Mutiny— the last years of the British Raj and first forty years of independence began increasingly to appear as part of the same historical period the idea of freedom has gone everywhere in India. Independence was worked for by people more or less at the top; the freedom it brought has worked its way down. People everywhere have ideas now of who they are and what they owe themselves. The processes quickened with the economic development that came after independence. What was hidden in 1972, or not easy to see, what perhaps was only in a state of becoming has become clearer. The liberation of spirit that has come to India could not come as release alone. In India with its layer below layer of distress and cruelty it had to come as disturbance. It had to come as a rage and revolt. India was now a country of a million little mutinies.

People are now caught in wave of change where they are prepared to commit any upheaval. We hope it would also happen with the act of empowerment. We look to the comprehension and cognition of people regarding the benefits of development and privileges which the Constitution has given to them.

Safeties and Securities

The Constitution provides certain safeties and securities to the scheduled tribes. About 50 years have passed since these reservations are granted to them. We wade a general enquiry about the benefits which are due to them. As a matter of fact the benefits are individual beneficiary programmes and the infrastructural programmes of link road, drainage, rural water supply and availability of fuels. I happen to meet Kodri, a resident of a village of Similwara Panchayat Samiti. We were walking together. We were together to catch a bus at the link road. I asked her: 'for you this must have been a usual exercise. Why don't you persuade the government to link this road to state roadways? It is hardly 3 km.' Her reply was prompt: '*Behnji*, today I am not carrying any load on my head. When we go to the neighbouring town, we carry either our farm produce or something else to be sold in the market. Generally it is heavy and we carry it on our head. During summer months it becomes very difficult to carry this load over such long distance. Last time I had my son Bhorroo, he had to be dragged all through the way. I took him for treatment'.

There are a large number of Kodries in TSP area. They suffer and they know their suffering but they are neither aware about the infrastructural facilities nor are they trained to meet the authorities to redress their complaints. I had elaborate talks with Kodri. She does not know about the rights that has been given to her—as a woman and as a tribal—by the Constitution. As a matter of fact neither the government nor the N.G.O. make it a point to educate the village women. Surprisingly enough Kodri and her counterparts in the neighbouring villages have attended the adult classes. She knows how to write her name. But the interesting thing is that she has never been taught by the organisers of adult classes to know some of the basic things about their very existence.

We have yet another encounter in Chittorgarh Tehsil. There is a programme in TSP area which gives financial assistance for self employment. We just wanted to meet a few people, male or female who had obtained some financial assistance for *Swarozgar* — self-employment. The Samiti authorities claimed that they had dispersed loans for self-employment. But they could not give any identification of the beneficiary. We moved in darkness, made our own enquiries and could catch hold of such beneficiaries. One was the cycle repair shop owner and second was, a tribal woman was sewing clothes of the local people. What about them: did they know their rights? Yes, they knew it. In fact they had been knocking at the doors of the BDO to get such a loan. She was given a large number of excuses: 'the grants have not come; if the grants come you will be the first beneficiary.' I approached someone whom I know for the sanction of grant. And finally my case was finalised I had to grease the hand of two officers and then the machine was sanctioned. There was a problem with the machine. The people of our locality suggest that the machine is local stuff and would break down any time. She explains: 'How do I understand this kind of development work'. The important work is that in the case of Kodri she did not know about infrastructural facilities but in the case of *machine wali bai* she knew her rights very well. But she got the machine with great difficulties.

There is yet another interesting case of two tribal boys. One had passed his B.A. with a training in education. In other words he was B.A., B.Ed. I met him in the hills of Aranod Partapgarh. Another boy who also happen to be from the same Panchayat, was a diploma holder in civil engineering. Both these youths were tribals. And were unemployed for the last two years. After making all the enquiries regarding their employment possibilities, I found that they were familiar with the reservation that they had been granted. Then, how did they not get any opportunity for any job? The answer is revealing and intriguing. One who was diploma holder made a bold statement:

> My father is a poor man. Somehow he got an inspiration to send me to a Polytechnic College I got my admission at Vidya Bhawan Polytechnic. During my stay I used to get Rs. 500 from my father in addition to ration. I prepared my own meals. When I completed my studies I thought it was the end of the tunnel for my father. But this did not happen.
>
> Not that no vacancy was filled in my area. But I did not have the financial resources to give to the officers. Those of our tribals who are well placed, elites, political workers they grabbed the position and I am still in waiting.

Similar is the statement of the person who had completed his B.Ed. We are now at a stage of development among tribals where more and more youths are coming forward after taking vocational and professional degrees. Now the employment market is over-crowded. The tribals, though they have reservation for the jobs and they know about it, they are still not able to get a suitable job for themselves. It appears awareness about reservation, employment have come but it has come very late. We just loudly think about the empowerment. The point is that even if women are empowered at the Panchayat and Zila Parishad, what can they do? There is no place for them. True, empowerment makes a woman to wield her power but to whom to wield power. These are some of the questions which needs to be raised and answered also.

Factionalism

We did not frame any questions to know about the prevalence of factionalism at different levels of Panchayati Raj tiers. We did not do it intentionally. It is because of the fact that people normally do not talk about factions in a tier. But it is a well-known fact that since the coming of the role of political parties in Panchayati Raj, factionalism has come. In a democracy factions are common but when the factions are characterised by kinship ties it harms the unity of the tribal society.

Traditionally we have mentioned earlier that village unity was a pervasive feature of rural India. The unity of village was never divisioned. When the party politics came in general and state elections in particular, there appeared cracks in village unity. What is damaging is that the tribals all over the world are a kin society. Clan and kinship keep the tribal society united. Tribals have fought against other villages on the basis of kin and clan conflict. But in the Panchayati Raj we have found that in order to get individual beneficiary programmes, the tribal kins have stood one against another. On the other hand factionalism is much dominating in the field of infrastructural facilities. Let us take the case of Gathol of Banswara district. Gathol village was sanctioned three hand pumps and all these were installed in a Baniya dominated locality. This was unacceptable to the tribals. They declared that the Baniyas would not fetch water from these hand pumps and if that happens the Bhils would cut their legs at night. The Baniyas got scared of tribals. A compromise was effected and additional three hand pumps were installed in tribal locality. This kind of factionalism has divided the whole village in tribal and non-tribal.

The point is when the women get empowerment will it be possible for them to thwart this kind of factionalism. Our feeling is that the tensions of this kind would not be faced with any strength by women. Our argument is that it is always goody goody to say that women have been empowered in the Panchayat Samiti. It is really a good observation to make that the women are in one-third of the total strength of Panchayati Raj. Our understanding of field suggest something else. Despite the numerical strength of tribal women they do not have prerequisites which can enable them to do something substantial. Despite this hypothetical observation we took up the task of assessing the awareness level of the members of sample group. We take a part view of this kind of data also that we have generated in the field.

Power Structure

The members to the Gram Panchayat and Panchayat Samiti have been given certain powers such as legislative, administrative, financial and judicial. It is expected of the elected members to be familiar with these powers. Even if they do not know the literary aspects of power at least the members should have some idea that in different fields of administration they can do and undo certain things. Even if the members fail to wield the power, they should at least demonstrate that they know everything. That goes a long way in creating discipline in the Panchayat Samiti.

In a broader plan the field data suggest that compared to females the males are far ahead in knowledge of administrative matters. This is understandable. There is more literacy among men than women. It is also said that women are so much preoccupied with household work that they do not get opportunity to devote time for Panchayat Samiti. And add to it women are first entrants to PRI. They have yet to learn about the procedures. The data are given at Table 7.1.

Table 7.1
Familiarity with Administrative Powers

Kind of Power	*Male*			*Female*		
	Yes	*No*	*Total*	*Yes*	*No*	*Total*
Legislative	21 (70%)	9 (30%)	30	14 (20%)	56 (80%)	70
Administrative	9 (30%)	21 (70%)		07 (10%)	63 (90%)	70
Financial	15 (50%)	15 (50%)	30	07 (10%)	63 (90%)	70
Judicial	18 (60%)	12 (40%	30	21 (30%)	49 (10%)	70

If a careful study of the development programmes implemented in the Tribal Sub-Plan Area is made it would at once become clear that a multiple scheme are in operation. The individual beneficiary programmes cover all the benefits which are required for educational development. It includes free hostel facilities, open school facilities and encouragement for games and sports. Even if a candidate happens to go outside the state for study, he is financially supported. Female students have not to pay their fees. There are individual beneficiary programmes for undergoing training of professional kind. There is stipend for those who take to STC, B.Ed., nursing, ITI, Foodcraft and Stockman. Similar are the schemes for providing resources for irrigation. There are facilities for digging a common well for a cluster of peasants, there is a PVC pipe scheme, watershed management, anicut and other such community water lifts programmes. What is important for women is that there are certain programmes which are specially meant for the welfare of women. It is globally known that women in general lack in nutritional food. They are also required to look into the integrated development of child. The schemes are taken on priority basis.

One of the schemes which has great relevance for women is Integrated Child Development Services. The scheme provides a package of services namely, supplementary nutrition, immunisation, health check referral services, nutrition and health education for per school children through *Anganwaries*. Yet another scheme is applied in nutrition programme. The scheme encourages the production and consumption of nutritive food in rural areas. In its wider aspects it includes horticulture, poultry, fisheries and minor irrigation. The UNICEF has assisted a special scheme for women and children development in the district of Banswara and Udaipur. The scheme aims to organise groups of women members to increase their income generating activities. Women are formed into groups and each group is trained in various vocations of craftsmanship. There is a programme of District Tribal Women Agency. The objective of the scheme is to identify programmes of crucial importance of tribal women's development and to create mechanism for conveying these programme for the benefit of tribal women. The main emphasis of these agencies are on education, training, health, nutrition, family welfare, economic development and employment of tribal women. An institutional framework has also been created. At the best level, there is a Mahila Vikas Kendra for every Gram Panchayat under the charge of a *Sathin* for supervision, there is one supervisor called *Pracheta* for one group of *Kendra*. Under education and training, non-formal education of girls, training courses for improving skills of family occupation is given.

Sericulture is yet another project which has attraction for women. Besides all this there are some special schemes exclusively meant for women. There is a provision for training of general nurses and compounders. There are girls' hostels made for women only. These hostels are provided in the form of Ashram schools. Then there are women ITI which provide training in tailoring and cutting trade. Specific women programmes are also covered by Saraswati Yojna and development of women education.

There is enough bewilderment in the programmes of tribal development specially meant for women. There is enough scope for confusion. The overlapping of benefits is so pervasive that the simple village women gets confused. It appears that in their enthusiasm of tribal development a number of schemes have been floated. Our fear is that with a large number of schemes the benefits go to the organisers rather than the beneficiaries. We put a simple question to our women respondents of sample group. The framers of programmes might be confused. But the respondents are not. A little less than one-fourth of women respondents are aware about some of the women development programmes. Interestingly a larger part of women have no knowledge about the availability of any such programme. Is it not a tragedy that there are about 50 development programmes specially made for women development and an overwhelming part of women for whom the programmes are meant do not know anything about it. How does the development authority work? And what is this empowerment of women which debarred them to keep ignorant about the schemes meant for them. The reality is that only a few programmes of *Anganwari*, Integrated Child Development and *Sathin* work. The remaining programmes are left to the discretionary functioning of the development personnel. We have made the awareness of women clear.

Orientation to General Development Programmes

The TSP area has already implemented eight five year plans. It is interesting to evaluate the impact of this plan on the tribals of the area. It is found that the plan ran short of the expectation. The literacy rate among the tribals could not be raised. The problems of land alienation continue to plague the area even now there are cases in the court which have not been decided.

Admittedly there are a large number of development programmes in the TSP area. They have a common focus to improve the lifestyle of people in such a way that they can very well involve themselves in the national mainstream. The programmes want to reduce the incidences of poverty and unemployment if, that is made possible, inequalities among groups of people will be minimised. Yet another objective of development programmes is to provide and strengthen the infrastructure in the villages and reduce exploitation. There is no disagreement about some of these objectives of five year plans. Our enquiries made on this account bring out very positive results. The women and the Ward Panchas have this much of cognition about the development programmes.

In fairness to the development agencies, the NGOs and the tribals we must admit that despite spending millions of money on development, though there is no material output corresponding to it, we are certain about one thing. People have gained a kind of a subjective consciousness which makes them great. An ordinary woman who works in the field thinks that she is a superstar. She knows that she is a tribal and tribals are taken seriously by the government. Though she herself does not know if some one inflicts harm to her, what can she do. No, she does not know anything. But she knows it for certain that she has privileges and there is a Constitution which protects her. This subjective hegemony that she has developed is the net gain of the development programmes.

Discrimination Against Man: Insider and Outsider

When we dwell on the theme of empowerment, basically we are concerned with gender relations. Does empowerment put women on an equal footing with men in the society? Our argument is that granting empowerment through legislation would not improve age-old discrimination which women in rural India are encountering. What is required of women is that they should be conscious enough about the privileges granted to them. We have found in Panchayat Samiti and Zila Parishad meetings that one-third strength of women does not make any material change in deciding the matter. As the democratic process go one has to toe the party line in such matters. And then whatever special provisions made for women in development programmes, interests everybody. What men would not like free education for their daughters? What men would not like integrated child development? What men would vote against nutritional *Nashta* given to the kids? There are all matters which do not divide men and women members in the Panchayat meetings. In such a situation the one-third majority does not make any watershed.

What is interesting is that the women should develop their own cognition about their own needs. The promoters of non-formal education have often been saying that the villagers are never weak in their wisdom. They understand their reality. But they are not articulate enough to express their desires. They have a culture of silence. They have eyes but they cannot see. They have legs but they cannot walk. They have land on which they work, day in and day out but they do not own the land. This is a kind of reality which cannot be comprehended only by passing a legislation in the assembly. We have tried to understand the comprehension of tribal women in terms of the reality of their society. There are enough institutional instances which vividly show that women are discriminated against men. We would show here the level of cognition which the tribal women have about their own society.

Discrimination, theoretically is at two levels in a tribal society. Women come in contact as daughter, wife, mother, widow, aged person with men of their own society. The interactions at this level are focussed on persons who are insiders. They are from their family, kin group, village, and *pal*. The gender relations with the insiders are also observed in the statutory and secular organisations as the Panchayat Samiti and Zila Parishad. The persons in the Samiti with whom they rub their shoulders are members of their own tribe. They are insiders.

But the moment a tribal woman goes to a market to dispose off her surpluses she is in contact with a trader who does not belong to her tribe. When she goes to school, at Panchayat Samiti office, her contacts are with outsiders. Women and girls who work on contract labour have to work with the overseers, engineers, *mats* and supervisors. Here again the contact is with the outsiders. The fact of the matter is that a woman in her gender relations comes in contact with both insiders and outsiders. Does her empowerment which is statutory influence her gender relations with insiders and outsiders. In the remaining part of this chapter we will discuss the cognition level of women and their mindset in empirical situation.

Equal Pay for Equal Work

Tribal women are now subjected to a secular democratic and socialist society which is held together by Constitution. Every law and order is subject to the approval of Constitutional framework. The state does not discriminate among individuals on the basis of caste, creed and sex. Sex here does not mean physical sex relations that would be vulgar. By sex the Constitution means gender, in other words, in the eyes of Law, in the eyes of state both men and women are equal. There cannot be any discrimination. The state has taken steps to permit women in occupations which were historically considered to be untouchable. Women are now in army, they are in air force and they are taking up professional courses such as engineering, in larger numbers is praiseworthy. But the beneficiaries to such openings are the women belonging to higher classes of society. Competition though open has certain prerequisites and the higher classes can afford to prepare their wards for such competitions. The tribal women lag behind. It would be wonderful to find out how many tribal girls have succeeded in entering into military and air force.

What concerns a tribal women in her day-to-day life is the discrimination she faces at the hands of contractor. It is written on the wall in the Tribal Sub-Plan Area that the minimum wages for labour for men and women are different. In the labour market of Dungarpur and Banswara the wages of a male at a construction site is Rs. 50 per day, for a women it is Rs. 40 whereas state approved maximum wages go upto Rs. 60. We had a very interesting anecdote with the women of Banswara. Some twenty years back when the Mahi Bajaj Sagar Dam was under construction the contractor practised the differential rate of wages to the thousands of women labourers. One of the courageous woman labourer took a fancy to write a simple post card to the State High Court. The State High Court in Public Interest Litigation (PIL) had listed the case. And by a decision of the court lakhs of rupees were paid on the principle of equal pay for equal work.

Empowerment can do this miracle. Though no stone would be unturned in the meetings of the Panchayat Samiti by the one-third women majority, surely many stones would be turned in the wider society if proper empowerment is given to women. What we argue is that there is need to bring a change in gender relations with outside world. The cognition and the mind set of people have to be aroused and our guess is that by attending the Panchayat Samiti meetings, and perhaps doing up-down between the village and the Tehsil or district headquarters tribal women would enhance their level of cognition.

We take yet another instance of gender relations from outsiders. The tribals have all through the ages being exploited by caste Hindu traders and government officials. The forest guard and the police constable had always an uninterrupted access to tribal women. They were ill-treated, oppressed, their modesty was exploited and they were occasionally raped. The tribal society at its level also developed an institutional cold shoulder against such sexual exploitation. Abortion of child did not come in the way. At worse there was a little reduction in bride price. In other words rape and molestation got the sanction of the society.

There was exploitation also at the hands of caste Hindu traders. We must see that in any rebellion, upheaval or anguish the tribals have not injured the trader. The trader went freely through the dense forests quite unharmed by the tribals. But recently a realisation has come among the tribals that the traders is his first rate enemy. He charges interest at exorbitant rate. If opportunity allows, he would not hesitate to molest a tribal girl in his shop itself. This cognition is now getting mature. Our another guess is that the legislative empowerment would have its side effects in the economic life also. It would reduce exploitation.

Gender relations with the outsiders are characterised by historical forces. We have argued elsewhere that the tribal society is different from caste society. Castes are divided on the lines of hierarchy. Whereas the tribal society has more or less been egalitarian. The tribal society has no fixed occupation. Even today a tribal is adapt to work on anything. It is quite unlike the caste society. The feudal rulers considered the tribal women as their sources of sexual lust. Earlier there was a practice that whenever a Bhil married he brought his wife to *Rawla*. And if the *Thakur* has a fancy he used to consummate the marriage while keeping the young bride with him for any number of days he liked. Now this has ceased but the newly married couple is even today required to pay visit to *Rawla*. For all the high caste Hindus right from *Thakur* to village *Bania* a Bhil woman even today is considered to be a play girl. If the records of the public health centres are checked carefully one would find that in majority of cases tribal women suffer from sexually transmitted diseases. Add to it various skin diseases. The point which we stress is that in their contact with outsiders the tribal women get a discriminatory treatment. Will the enforced empowerment reduce this discrimination?

Gender Relations: Insiders

Tribal women is victimised not only by outsiders, she is also victimised by insiders. In their own society the women bear the heaviest burden. Earlier we have mentioned that it is they who manage the house and manage the finances. Men often indulge in gossips and liquor. Normally their work is over when sowing is done. The rest of the agricultural operations are looked after by women. And then, they do not have their say in matters of decision. In contemporary tribal society of south Rajasthan there has been a marked flow of tribals to urban and industrial community in search of jobs. One can find buses over occupied on days of festivals like Holi and Diwali from cities like Ahmedabad, Vadodra and Indore. A large number of tribals work in Gujarat. Normally they do the household work. Whatever be their name they are called *Ramla*. They have an association located at Ahmedabad, the strength of *Ramla* Association in terms of membership comes to twenty thousand.

When the *Ramla* migrate to Gujarat, who looks after their family at the parent village? Obviously the women. The female heads of tribal family in south Rajasthan are confronted with a conflict which is unhistorical and unconventional. The females live in *Pal*—a wilderness. They maintain the family. Their problems are several. There is an encroachment on land. There are miscreants who have their eyes on the young girls of the family. For a tribal female the situation is really terrible. But anyhow she maintains the status. In the context of empowerment the whole situation of the tribal female needs to be looked after.

There are certain institutions in the tribe which inferiorise the gender relations. It is inherent in the tribal system to look down the birth of a daughter. The brass plate — *thali* is rung only on the birth of a son. There is no vibration of brass at the birth of a daughter. She is aware of discrimination soon after her birth. And the tragedy of all tragedies is that it is she who brings bride wealth to parents and she is looked down.

Thus the gender relations with the insiders are guided by customary law. The institution of bride price has given a property concept to women. She is considered to be a property of the parent. They give her in marriage in consideration of bride price. And the groom or his parents who pay the bride price amount become the 'possessor' of the wife. She has to keep herself with the groom and the parents in all conditions and if she takes a fancy to run away with another husband, the bride price has to be compensated by the new husband. The amount of bride price is negotiable. Normally it is reduced. Such a state of customary law reduces the status of tribal women. For this the women has to develop a cognition about the institutional status.

The customary laws have yet another stigma attached to tribal women. She is in some unusual circumstances considered a witch. We have given a detailed note on the craft, the witch was supposed to tame the power of supernatural which empowers her to victimise any person she chooses. The victim of witchcraft can get inflictions of any disease. And there is no medical treatment of the disease inflicted. According to customary law, in such situations there is a hunt for the witch. If she is identified she has to pass tests of ordeals which are very severe. It is difficult for any human being to establish her innocence. The punishment to a witch is death by beating. The customary laws in this respect need serious review. What we argue is that there are a few customary laws which on one hand take the law of country in hand and on the other hand, reduce the status of women. The cases of elopement which are customary put the women to a status of commodity. A careful scanning of customary laws would show that a woman in a tribal society is not considered a human element with any degree of pride and dignity. She is taken up as an item of consumption, a commodity of possession. The institution or customary laws of bride wealth, elopement, abduction, very aptly show that she is not taken respectfully. Here is the area where women should develop their cognition, comprehension of their own status.

It is very common to find a woman in a very uncomfortable situation in a tribal family. Day in and day out her husband and even her sons mouth foul words in addressing her. Perhaps all conversation between the genders are characterised by dirt and filth. And the women consider it to be the approved way of interaction. She does not feel bad even if her own grown up sons abuse her.

Why women suffer so much at the hands of conversational conventions and customary laws? In their new status when a tribal woman adorns the chair of Zila Pramukh, any time her husband could step in and talked to her in the presence of all others in a filthy way. Enough is enough. There is enough room for mobilising the power of the women. She has to be made conscious about her rights and privileges. It is in this field of gender relations that the new status of tribal women has to be explored.

Reference

1. Naipaul, V.S., *India a Million Mutinies Now,* Rupa and Co., New Delhi, 1999, p. 517.

CHAPTER 8

Cultural Empowerment: Beyond Panchayati Raj

I

The major trend in social sciences today is to stress on culture. Interest in culture has emerged because of the strengthening of the process of globalisation. 'Cultural change', 'cultural modernisation', 'cultural imperialism' and 'cultural onslaught' are some of the new idioms which have become prevalent in social sciences. Even political scientists look at the political processes with an emphasis on cultural change. Culture emanates from the unity of human kind in nature. It situates itself as a meta-natural reality. It is manifested in the technological, mental, moral, social, aesthetics and spiritual achievements of human kind. Culture gives meaning to our relationship with the other. As it also forms our subjective identity. Culture, therefore, enters into the processes of social change in many forms and at various levels. It defines the quality of social change and its indicators. By selecting adaptations to outside cultural forces, it has a large measure of resistance. With all its historical pervasiveness, it has a core which acts as a filter or a moderator to the outside forces of cultural contact and change. This also explains why in each mainstream culture one may find existence of sub-culture and country cultures.

In connection with the analysis of empowerment of tribal women we take a different perspective. Our argument is that the tribals have their culture which is different from caste Hindu culture. It is this tribal culture which gives meaning to the relationships of empowerment to others. True Panchayati Raj legislation has empowered women. This enables tribal women to meet others. But the meaning to this meeting is given by the tribal culture. Second we want to stress one more point which requires a little elaboration, if there is a culture it also creates a counter culture. The tribals are surrounded by caste Hindus. The caste

Hindus have their culture which is characterised by the great tradition of Hinduism. This kind of great tradition oriented Hindu culture has become the mainstream culture of the tribal region. In the processes of development, and the provisions of constitutional safety and security and the measures of empowerment are manifest in Panchayati Raj have given emergence among tribals a kind of culture which is surely not Hindu culture but a counter culture. This counter culture is visible in the belief of the tribals in secularism and socialism. The counter culture of the tribals is further characterised in their efforts to protect their cultural identity.

K.S. Singh in the *People of India* has observed that despite the tribals orienting to Christianity and Hinduism expressed their unshakable faith in their local deities. No God—*Vishnu* or *Shiv* is higher to their *Bherujee. Bherujee* is accessible on all situations of emergency. It clearly shows that the tribal culture is basically a counter culture. A Bhil may have all respect and sympathy for Tazia, for Rishabhdev, for Gurudwara, but his primordial loyalty is towards his village deity or ancestral deity. His interest today is to maintain the identity and survival of this counter culture.

Our argument here is that the empowerment which has come to the tribal women though legislation is only one example of protecting her. If we look at the history of the tribal development in the TSP area we would find that enough has been made to give self-sufficiency to these people. By now they have not only taken to settled agriculture but have started taking three crops a year. They are not only growers of cereals they take to commercial crops and horticulture. If not green revolution in its fullest form, a part of it has come to tribals. It is very common to find a Bhil woman making a bargain of some thousands of rupees in the local market and she never makes a bad bargain. These are instances of economic empowerment. We want to examine empowerment in its wider dimension.

It should not be understood that empowerment is a monolith concept and affects only the behaviour of members in the Panchayati Raj. The powers that the tribal women get through the Panchayati Raj legislation largely remains restricted to the four walls of Panchayat Samiti. The ramification of empowerment are quite wide. As a matter of fact there is a linkage of Panchayati Raj empowerment with the matrix of power and cultural complexes at regional, state and national level. The dimensions of empowerment thus cut across Panchayat Samiti and Zila Parishad and take dimensions of cultural form. Yogendra Singh analyses the role of culture in the understanding of social change in contemporary India:[1]

> In the context of overall social change, it is essential to examine the nature of relationships that demands for cultural autonomy or ethnicity have with the processes of cultural integration in the Indian society as a whole. Sociological studies suggest that the existence of a viable linkage between these two otherwise contradictory processes cultural integration of diverse entities in the Pan-Indian Society has had a long history in India. Its matrix was that of a civilization. This civilization was not subsumed in, but out across religious, ethnic, linguistic and regional boundaries. It substanced upon interdependence among diverse plural social entities established through technology, production processes, trade, market and circulation of products and of personnel engaged in pursuits of craft, art, aesthetics, knowledge and learning.

Empowerment thus is comprehensive within the Panchayati Raj it has its only one dimension. This dimension is political. It may have certain economic and other benefits also. But beyond all this tribal women are exposed to a large number of forces. For instance women in urban communities and rural communities have witnessed a new kind of empowerment which has come from urbanisation, modernisation, industrialisation and general awakening. Women talk much about their newly acquired power sources. More and more women are entering colleges and universities. A new dress pattern has come. The dietary habit has undergone change and interestingly women from both rural and urban communities are talking about information technology. All these changes have come among women not because of some legislation passed in assembly or parliament. Modernisation has come due to new forces.

If modernisation has brought about changes in the rural and urban side, they have also changed the tribal women. They are no exception. The dress pattern of tribal women has witnessed changes, which do not permit tribal women to be distinguished from non-tribal women. Tribal men also have come on par with the non-tribal men in the dress pattern. In dietary habit a similar change has been observed. Banana and some inferior kind of apple have become popular fruits among the tribals. Earlier they only used to take *goord* as their sweet. But this has now been replaced by sweets mostly made of milk. Those who used to take country liquor have now developed a taste for Indian made foreign liquor.

The changes brought about by force of modernisation including education, urbanisation have made changes which overwhelmed the changes brought about by empowerment. It suggested that the non-legislative forces are more superior and powerful than the legislative forces.

It appears that the combined forces of empowerment along with constitutional safeties and securities and the forces of modernisation have given rise to a counter culture in tribal society. We shall have occasion to dwell on it when we have completed an analysis of the new interaction patterns experienced among the people. To find out the new patterns of interactions resulting from the combined forces of empowerment and modernisation we will examine certain case studies which we conducted during the field work.

Emerging Tribal Women Leadership: Harmi Bai Calls the Shots

In the earlier part of the chapter we have made a point that when women are empowered through legislation, they are likely to wield their power in the Panchayati Raj institutions and also beyond that. Our visit to the Tribal Sub-Plan Area has brought us in close relations with some of the tribal women. We definitely find them sparkling. We have developed a belief that if tribal women are given proper opportunities they might prove their worth to lead the society ahead. It is not that we have always found successful stories, there are stories which show the failure of the women in making a dent. In the pages that follow we shall highlight some of the successes and failures of tribal women. In describing the new situation we only want to stress the point that discrimination of women against men is not only a phenomenon of urban life. There is a latent growing evil among the tribal women who had long remained victims of the culture of science. If properly groomed their tongue can speak, their ears can hear and their legs can walk.

Hurmi Bai is a tribal women somewhere in the age group 35 - 40. She is a robust looking woman. She displays urban style of wearing *Sari.* Unlike the tribal women she wears a bindi and poses herself as a modern woman hailing from city. She is articulate in her conversation and makes a convincing speech. If she is given a theme she can immediately role play the same. She is of the kind of a modern leader who can very loudly raise slogans and respond to situations spontaneously.

However her earlier history has not been promising. She was married to a tribal man who was an agriculturist. But in the field of agriculture both of them have not been successful to make any breakthrough. All is traditional with the couple. Hurmi did not attend any school. There is no account of any formal education to her credit. She belongs to Kotra village which falls in the Panchayat Samiti of Kotra of Udaipur district. Kotra is situated at the western fringe of Udaipur city. It is close to the state roadways which links Udaipur to Mount Abu. Kotra is known for its remoteness. Some 50 years back Morris Cartiers of the fame of the book *The Twice Born* (MacMillan,1965) worked in Kotra Bhoomet, the description of tribals given by Cartiers present Kotra as an area of darkness. Real savage life was observed by him. So Hurmi Bai belongs to this anthropological region of south-western Rajasthan.

Hurmi Bai in a casual way came in contact with the social workers of *Aastha*—an NGO located at Udaipur. *Aastha* 'discovered' Hurmi Bai. In the beginning when the *Aastha* workers persuaded tribal women to come within the working programme of the agency, Hurmi Bai and others denied. For them, it was a design of the social workers to persuade them to go for tubectomy—the operation for sterilization. This suspicion worked successfully. And Hurmi Bai along with the other women never showed their face to *Aastha*. But for *Aastha,* it was not an end of their efforts. Hurmi Bai and others were convinced and they came in large numbers within the fold of *Aastha*. Such a move on the part of Hurmi Bai was looked with envy by the menfolk of Kotra. But Hurmi Bai and her friends had moved ahead. And there was no looking back.

At the time of our visit Hurmi headed Adivasi Jagran Manch, an organisation created with the support and blessings of *Aastha*. Now Hurmi has an appreciable following of women. Last time Hurmi Bai contested for the membership of Panchayat Samiti. The factional politics worked against her and despite her being a fire brand, she was defeated. But this did not discourage her. She moved her *Manch* ahead and at the instance of *Aastha* got an opportunity to visit Canada. She attends tribal conferences, meetings and seminars at regional and national levels. By now she has become quite articulate. She knows a little of reading and writing, enters into correspondence and is capable to talk with important persons.

What is the agenda of Hurmi Bai? What does her Adivasi Jagran Manch want? The questions are quite interesting. We had protracted talks with her. She says that tribal women have a potential. They have been subdued not only by the tribal men but by the non-tribal men also. And here she talks about gender relations. Her second objective is to mobilise the tribal men and women and to get the maximum benefit which is due to them. She considers non-tribals as the enemies of tribal society. She does not expect non-tribals to work for the welfare of the tribals.

True, Hurmi Bai has her agenda for working. She is not scared of the cover of forest which surrounds her and moves with her head high, day in and day out. But there are some personal tragedies also which she has to suffer. Her husband is a non-entity. Her economic position by any standard is not satisfactory. Her own daughter who is a teenager is married. She could not make any headway at the level of her family, husband and wife. Despite the shortcomings it establishes that if Hurmi Bai could make a dent into wider society, without having any schooling and economic support, there is a hope that more Hurmi Bais could emerge if the NGOs work with a sense of dedication.

The Sarpanch Fights with a System

Kanchan Devi Meena was the Sarpanch of Paduna Gram Panchayat of Jawar Tehsil. She is a middle-aged women belonging to the Meena tribe. She has passed her higher secondary examination. She is very much enthusiastic to work for Gram Panchayat. In her childhood she provided a little of leadership in her school. When she came to higher secondary she showed ample interest in the school union activities. Her parents though literate were sympathetic to her ambitions.

Kanchan contested elections for the Sarpanch. She won the election. She was very keen to do something for the cluster of villages which fall within Paduna Gram Panchayat. Before contesting for elections she had experience of working in the *Anganwari*. *Anganwari* of Paduna was rated high in the Panchayat because of her efforts. After being Sarpanch she took up the objective of implementing the programmes of TSP area. There has never been dearth of funds, if one is keen to implement the programmes. And it is the speciality of TSP area. The flow of funds normally in the scheduled area never ceases. Kanchan only wanted to implement her programmes.

She seriously worked on the development schemes. But the co-operation of the officials of Gram Panchayat was not forthcoming. Sometimes hurdles came from the Panchayat Samiti, at other times from the district development office. And technicalities had to be observed at every stage of the framing and implementation of programmes. In her case the Gram Sevak was expected to jointly sign the cheques with her. The Gram Sevak for one reason or the other took a back seat so far the implementation of the programmes was concerned. Kanchan was clear. She said that programmes must be brought to ground and red tapism would in course of time be reduced. She knocked at the doors of her superior officers. And succeeded in getting sanctions for some projects. When the sanction letters came, payment had to be made. At this stage the Gram Sevak refused to put his signature on the cheque. And this was enough to enrage Kanchan. In the height of her temper she slapped on the face of Gram Sevak. And the Gram Sevak was never a lesser mortal. He returned the slap and there appeared a bad scene in the Gram Panchayat office. This, however, did not discourage Kanchan. She has gone to the court.

Kanchan has moved the Panchayati Raj authorities. Her plea is different. She says that she is fighting against the system. If the officials or the government servant are not committed to the development of the Gram Panchayat nothing substantial can be done in the Gram Panchayat. Her argument is that as the elected representatives have a commitment to the region, so should the

marked as a pastoral land. The meeting of the Gram Panchayat decided that the encroachment may be vacated. She wanted help of the CEO. This help never came. On the other hand those who had encroached the land sent several threats to Geeta Devi. She was told that she would be eliminated. This made the working of the Sarpanch difficult.

The high caste Hindus were looking for an opportunity to bring no confidence motion against Geeta. The motion was tabled and she was defeated. Thus her departure from the Gram Panchayat was unceremonious.

There is yet another case of Gulab Devi Ravat. She was Sarpanch of Gram Panchayat Togi of Rajsamand District. The members of Gram Panchayat who were mostly high caste Hindus made the working of Sarpanch very difficult. On one pretext or other a no confidence motion was put by the Panchayat members. On one occasion when a no confidence motion had to be put for voting, her supporters were kidnapped and she was defeated. But this would not deter her. She went to the High Court and got the no confidence vacated. But the members had decided not to allow her to work. She had already spent Rs. 50 thousand on litigation and no confidence motion was again moved against her. And this time she was defeated. She argues that those who voted against her were not qualified members. But the fact remains that she ceased to be a Sarpanch.

Tribal Woman is Always Vulnerable as Accused

We have observed elsewhere that the value of virginity is comparatively weak among tribal women. If a woman is found deviating from sexual modesty the only penalty which she has to suffer is the loss of some amount in the traditional bride wealth. In such a situation a tribal woman is not much vulnerable so far as strict observance of virginity is concerned. Perhaps one very strong allegation which a woman has to suffer is of her being a witch. Once a woman is alleged to be a witch she becomes a victim of a large number of complaints.

The tribal Ward Panch of Banswara district belonging to Wagtalab is well-known in the TSP area. The media played it even out of proportion. It so happened that the Ward Panch on one night was retiring after her evening meals that a gang of four persons entered her house and they declared that she was a witch. All the milch cattle of the village have dried because of her. Most of the children of the village had suffered one disease or the other. She was responsible for the crisis in the village. The Ward Panch denied the charges but the gang dragged her out of house and threatened her to behead her. However, this could not be done but the poor Ward Panch had to quit the job. Her husband had to leave the Panchayat and go in exile.

It is our common observation that the Panchayat members normally declare a woman Panch, Sarpanch or Pradhan to be loose in sexual behaviour. She is victimised by a number of allegations and it makes difficult for women member to perform her job. Though character assassination is not a serious thing among tribal women, but it makes the atmosphere muddy and murky. The friendly situation for proper functioning is normally non-existent.

Women Initiate Tribal Social Reform

The tribal society is not an hierarchical society. On the other hand it is a society which largely runs on tribal traditions and customary laws. Some of the customs and traditions of the tribe are derogatory. If the tribal women have to improve their life style on par with men, some of the social evils have to be reformed. The women are required to be empowered outside the corridors of Panchayati Raj, to the family and village.

During our visits we found that in the Pai village of Udaipur district a voluntary organisation has emerged which is known as 'Mahila Jagratee Sanstha'. The office bearers of the institute are all Bhil women. The Institute gets its inspiration from *Aastha,* the NGO of Udaipur city. The institute has a programme of social reform. It wants its stands to attain autonomy for the village. In such a village liquor would be prohibited, non-vegetarian diet would be a taboo. The office-bearers have a good following. It appears that in course of time the institute would be able to do some good job in the field of social reform.

Women Too are Corrupt

It has been a general understanding in the Tribal Sub-Plan area that the tribal women non-officials do not accept any underhand money for doing a work. This has been proved wrong. There is enough empirical evidence to suggest that women more often than not grease their palm. A large number of women non-officials are chargesheeted for accepting bribe. Fixed amounts are determined for doing particular kinds of work. In the case of appointment of Panchayat Samiti jobs the bribe money is said to be quite observant, something more than 20 to 30 thousands. Corruption among the women has become a common characteristic. And if one comes clean in her behaviour the survival is doubtful. As a matter of fact the decision-making in the Gram Panchayat and Panchayat Samiti is not directly through women members. In many of the cases it is prompted by male members. In such a situation the intermediaries accept the bribe. And if a woman member displays some boldness, all underhand practices are employed to oust her.

II

Empowerment is a concept which has become much popular today. It has almost become fashionable not only in social sciences but in the contemporary political vocabulary the term is very common. The protagonists of gender issues also use it as a household word. The impression created in the masses is that if women are given proper empowerment, most of their problems would be solved. Empowerment seems to be a prescription given to all women notwithstanding their ethnic and hierarchical status. The present study consists several of these common observations. The empirical reality as we have found among the tribals of south Rajasthan does not conform to many of the popular generalisations. It appears much of politics is made out of it. There is an agitation from women to get reservation in the parliament. In its enthusiasm the parliament has passed Seventy-Third Constitutional Amendment by giving more powers to women in Panchayati Raj. The state governments including the government of Rajasthan has assumed that many of the problems of tribal women would be solved by empowering women. So much so good.

In giving empowerment we have very conveniently forgotten that the prerequisites which are needed for the success of empowerment are very fragile. The state of Rajasthan made a mistake by accepting decentralisation of power in 1959. But the scheme succumbed and the feudal structure of Rajasthan society failed, Panchayati Raj miserably. The lesson of history the state government forgot and it has taken to a new Panchayati Raj Act which provides reservation to one-third of the members at all levels of Panchayati Raj. However, the prerequisites are poor and the performance of the women members has been weak.

Do Rajasthan women require empowerment? The question may be considered absurd. Why women should not be empowered, when all over the world they are treated as subalterns. But our answer is not complete. We shall qualify it. It must be stated that the status of tribal women at least in south Rajasthan is different from the status of women in rural Rajasthan or urban Rajasthan. Historically, tribal women have enjoyed a status which does not meet any significant discrimination. We have stated earlier that there is no straight jacket type division of labour in tribal society. A woman might bring water and the man grind corns, a woman might clean the cattle shed and the man keep vigil on the crop. A perfect freedom is seen in the division of labour in a tribal society.

The only discrimination which is glaring in the tribal society is that of bride wealth. This differentiation is also being reduced in the case of *Bhagats*. At the level of marriage there is no element of religion. A tribal marriage is essentially a social contract. The moment a woman wants to dissolve marriage she has only to manage for the return of the bride wealth. The tribal bride is never frightened with the horror of burning. She has not to pass the life of a widow which the Hindu women face at Varanasi or Vrindavan. It is a different thing that in her advanced age she is constrained to live in widowhood. In the field of economy also it is she who makes the best of a bargain. What is important is that the gender relations in the tribal society are not characterised by any conspicuous discrimination.

On the other hand it should also be stressed that gender relations in the tribal society are not homogenous. The tribals who have taken to government jobs, accepted political life and have settled in urban areas and encounter a degree of discrimination. Economy, politics and education have introduced the variable of discrimination in tribal society. The need for empowerment of women in tribal society, therefore, is for those women who have some education, some job, some discrimination. In other words the masses of tribal women living in the higher land hardly have any prick of discrimination. Do such women require empowerment? It is possible that in the near future when tribal society gets a complicated stratification, it might need an input of empowerment. But this too might be a hurried statement.

On the strength of our empirical data it could be safely said that whatever gender issues in terms of empowerment that we find in tribal society do not originate from their religion. In the caste society and also what we call the national society, the gender issues stem from religious fundamentalism. If we happen to scan the observations of women studies and popular women writers, we would immediately find that the discrimination is from the religious texts. A wife is considered to be inferior because in the Hindu scripture she is considered as such. She is a widow. She is a divorcee. She is beaten. And the Hindu scriptures are more than several. What is justified in one scripture is repudiated in another. At one place it is stated that where women reside the Gods dwell and at other place says that women do not understand any language other than filth and beating. Contradictions in scriptures abound. And this results in the inferiorisation of women.

The tribal women do not face such a religious dilemma. Their relations are traditional. Admittedly they are addressed in a foul language, they get beating also but on major events of life, discrimination is minimised with them.

When the tribal women are empowered in the Panchayati Raj we find the actual power at the grass-root level is wielded by insiders, outsiders, high castes, political bosses and bureaucrats. The net gain of the so-called tribal Panch, Sarpanch and Pradhan is the confrontation with the bureaucracy, official technicality and court litigation. The fact of the matter is that the women are exploited by a number of people both within the Panchayati Raj framework and outside it.

A new trend is visible. The Bharatiya Janata Party and its cultural wings such as Vishva Hindu Parishad, Jagaran Manch, Bajrang Dal and a host of other organisations having allegiance with fundamentalism are working in the tribal area through educational institutions, hostels and Rashtriya Swayamsevak Sangh (RSS) to convert the tribals to wider Hinduism. Tribal women are told time and again that they are Hindus. The new image bestowed on tribal women is increasingly motivating them to take to the model of Hindu women for their imitation. When this processes begin to give multiple results the tribal women would suffer from all those evils which afflict the Hindu women today.

It appears that with the coming of Seventy-Third Amendment and the consequent reservation in Panchayati, Raj, the tribal women are passing through a transitional stage. On one hand they are given reservation with a kit full of power. And on the other hand the women do not fulfil the prerequisites which are required for a proper wielding of power. This is what we precisely mean by transitional stage. It is only recently that the NGO country report on 'plus 5' has brought out the observation of Task Force on Women 2000: India. This report is also critical of the policy statement on women's empowerment incorporated in the Ninth Plan which 'boxes women and girl's into five simplistic categories reflecting little understanding of the rights of women and their potential as people and citizens'.

Admittedly the Panchayati Raj has given power to tribal women. But it is the nature of power that it is grabbed. If the women while away their time, others would grab it. And it would be the women's fault if others wield power assigned to them. Nalini Rajan (*Secularism, Democracy, Justice,* Sage, 1998) has a very positive advise to women at this juncture of history when she is at the doorstep of power:

> Rather she must assert her right to fight and possess other kinds of rights as well along with them. Yes, biological differences matter, but only upto a point.

Bibliography

A. Books

D.L. Sheth and Ashis Nandy (ed.), *The Multiverse of Democracy*, New Delhi, 1966.

Berman Jan, *Of Peasants, Migrants and Paupers*, Oxford University Press, Delhi, 1985.

Ranajit Guha (ed.), *Subaltern Studies*, V, Oxford University Press, Delhi, 1977.

K.S. Singh (ed.), *Tribal Situations in India*, Centre of Advanced Studies, Shimla, 1964, New Delhi, 1986 (reprint).

———, (ed.), *Tribal Movement in India*, Vols. I & II, Manohar, New Delhi, 1982.

G.S. Ghurye, *Caste and Race in India*, Popular Prakashan, Bombay, 1979.

D.N. Majumdar, *Races and Cultures of India*, Universal Publishers, Lucknow, Kalyani Publishers, New Delhi, 1990 (reprint).

Pareek, R.N., *The People of India*, Orient Books Reprint, New Delhi.

———, *Tribal Culture in Flux*, B.R. Publication Corporation, 1977.

Yogendra Singh, *Modernisation of Indian Tradition*, Thomas Press, 1973.

B.N. Yogendhar and Amitav Mukherjee (ed.), *Reading in Decentralised Planning*, Concept, New Delhi, 1991.

D.S. Chaudhary, *Emerging Rural Leadership in Indian State*, Delhi, 1981.

K.S. Padhy and P.P. Tripathy, *Voting Behaviours of Tribals in India*, Delhi, 1994.

Berthol Kuhn, *Participatory Development in Rural India*, Radiant Publishers, 1998.

R.S. Gautam (ed.), *Panchayati Raj in Madhya Pradesh*, (Hindi), MPISSR, Ujjain, 1998.

K. Maithreyi Raj, *Women's Study in India: Some Perspectives*, Popular Prakashan, Bombay, 1986.

Renuka Pamecha, *Elite in Tribal Society*, Rupa, Jaipur, 1985.

Rajni Kothari (ed.), *Caste in Indian Politics*, Orient Longman, New Delhi, 1970.

———, *Democratic Polity and Social Change in India's Crisis and Opportunities*, Allied Publishers, New Delhi, 1976.

Sushila Agarwal, *Status of Women*, Rupa, Jaipur, 1994.

Sushila Patni, *Women Political Elite Search for Identity*, Rupa, Jaipur, 1994.

Vijay Kaushik, *Women's Movement and Human Rights*, Pointer Publishers, Jaipur, 1997.

P.C. Mehta, *Changing Face of Bhils*, Shiva Publishers, Udaipur, 1998.

Hoy Dewid Coufens, *Foucault: A Critical Reader*, Bessil Blackwell, 1992.

Crook Stephen and Others, *Post-Modernisation*, Sage, London, 1993.

Lewis Couser and Bernard, *Sociological Theory*, (4th Edition), MacMillan, New York, 1976.

T.H. Eriksen, *Small Place, Large Issues*, Pluto Press, London, 1905.

Gurew Saneja, *Feminist Knowledge: Critiques and Construct* (ed.), Routledge, 1990.

G.S. Graval and Hugh Jobston (ed.), *The India-Canada Relationship* (Exploring the Political, Economic and Cultural Dimensions), Sage, New Delhi, 1994.

K.S. Singh, *The Scheduled Tribes*, People of India, National Series, Vol. III, Oxford University Press, Calcutta, 1997.

Moris Godlier, *Perspectives in Marxists Anthropology*, Cambridge, London, 1978.

Arundhati Roy, *The Greater Common God*, India Book, Bombay, 1999.

George Mathews, *Status of Panchayati Raj in India*, Concept, New Delhi, 1995.

Wendy Warcourt, *Feminist Perspective on Sustainable Development*, Zed Books, London and New Jersey, 1994.

Sneja Gurew, *Feminist Knowledge, Critique and Construct*, Routledge, London, 1990.

Shirin-M. Rai and Livesley Geraldine (eds.), *Women and the State: International Perspective*, London, 1996.

Gerda Lerner, *The Creation of Patriarchy*, Oxford, London, 1998.

Chandra Tarapade Mohenty and Rueso Curdes, *Third World Women and the Feminism*, Indiana, Bloomington, 1991.

Neera Desai and Maithrey Krishnaraj, *Women and Society in India*, Ajanta, New Delhi, 1987.

Shaheed Amin and Dipesh Chakraburty, *Subaltern Studies IX*, Oxford, London, 1996.

Leela Dube, Women and Kinship: *Comparative Perspectives on Gender in South and South East Asia*, Vistaar, New Delhi, 1997.

I.P. Desai (ed.), *History of Rural Development in Modern India*, II, New Delhi, 1977.

V.S. Naipaul, *India: A Million Mutinies Now*, Rupa and Co., New Delhi, 1990.

B. Research Papers and Articles

Andre Beteille, 'Empowerment', *Economic and Political Weekly*, March 6-13, 1999, p. 590.

Indu Agnihotri, Vina Mazumdar, 'Changing Terms of Political Discourse', *Economic and Political Weekly*, July 22, 1995, p. 1869.

B.C. Mehta, 'Gender and Regional Pattern of Work Participation in Rural Rajasthan', *Man Power Journal*, Vol. XXXV, No. 2, July - September, 1999, p. 23.

K.S. Singh, 'Hinduism and Tribal Religion: An Anthropological Perspective', *Man In India*, 1993.

Gate Omvedt, 'Unfair Label', *The Hindu*, Sunday, February 13, 2000.

G.S. Swamawat, 'Development of Tribal Women as a Part of Human Resource Development', *Tribe*, Vol. 28.

Vidhuty Mohanty, 'Panchayati Raj, Seventy-Third Constitutional Amendment and Women', *Economic and Political Weekly*, December 13, 1995.

Beena Agarwal, 'Work Participation of Rural Women in Third World: Some Data and Conceptual Biases', *Economic and Political Weekly*, December 21-29, 1985.

Poornima Vyasulu, 'Women in Panchayati Raj: Grass Roots Democracy in Malgudi', *Economic and Political Weekly*, December 25, 1999.

Amar Kumar Singh, 'Status of the Tribals in India', *Social Change*, Vol. 23, No. 2-3, July-September 1993, p. 5.

P.K. Bhomic, 'The Development Approach to Adivasi Problem', *Adivasi*, Vol. XVI, No. 2, Bhubaneshwar, 1976.

Arjun Patel, 'Hinduisation of Adivasis: A Case of South Gujarat', *Indian Journal of Secularism*, Vol. I, No. 1, April - June, 1997.

C. Reports and Government Publications

Census of India, 1961, 1971, 1981 and 1991. Series 18, Rajasthan, Parts XIII, A and B: Village and Town Director, Village and Town-wise Primary Census Abstract, District Census Handbook, Banswara, Dungarpur, Udaipur, Chittorgarh Districts, Director of Census Operation Rajasthan.

The National Sample Survey No. 126th, 9th, 11th, 12th, and 13th Rounds, May 1995 to May 1998: Government of India, Cabinet Secretariat, 1962.

National Perspective Plan.

All India Women's Conference, Annual Reports.

National Committee on Women's Education.

National Women's Commission's Report.

Women's Development Project: Rajasthan, May 1985.

Government of Rajasthan, Department of Rural Development and Panchayati Raj.

Index